SCHOOL LIBRARIANSHIP SERIES

Edited by Diane de Cordova Biesel

1. *Reference Work in School Library Media Centers: A Book of Case Studies,* by Amy G. Job and MaryKay Schnare, 1996.
2. *The School Library Media Specialist as Manager: A Book of Case Studies,* by Amy G. Job and MaryKay W. Schnare, 1997.

The School Library Media Specialist as Manager

A Book of Case Studies

Amy G. Job and MaryKay W. Schnare

School Librarianship Series, No. 2

Scarecrow Press, Inc.
Lanham, Md., & London
1997

SCARECROW PRESS, INC.

Published in the United States of America
by Scarecrow Press, Inc.
4720 Boston Way
Lanham, Maryland 20706

British Library Cataloguing in Publication Information Available

Library of Congress Cataloging-in-Publication Data

Job, Amy G.
The school library media specialist as manager : a book of case studies / Amy G. Job and MaryKay W. Schnare.
p. cm. — (School librarianship series ; no. 2)
Includes bibliographical references and index.
ISBN 0-8108-3363-8 (alk. paper)
1. School libraries—United States—Administration. 2. Instructional materials centers—United States—Management. I. Schnare, W. MaryKay, 1945- . II. Title. III. Series.
Z675.S3J62 1997
025.1′978—dc21 97-20841
CIP

ISBN 0-8108-3363-8 (pbk. : alk. paper)

♾ ™ The paper used in this publication meets the minimum requirements of American National Standard for Information Sciences—Permanence of Paper for Printed Library Materials, ANSI Z39.48–1984.
Manufactured in the United States of America.

Contents

Series Editor's Foreword

The works in the School Librarianship Series are directed toward the library school professor, the library school student, and the district supervisor. Each volume examines the role of the school library media specialist as an agent of change within the educational system, with the goal of exploring the philosophical basis of school librarianship yesterday, today, and tomorrow.

Site-based management, the challenges of technology, and multiculturalism are a few of the current educational issues presented in *The School Library Media Specialist as Manager: A Book of Case Studies.* The authors present realistic situations, and thought-provoking questions at the end of each case study engage the reader in a search for possible solutions to the problems presented.

Diane de Cordova Biesel
Series Editor

Preface

The challenge facing the library media specialist is to design and deliver an effective library media program. Faced with the impact of technology, societal pressures, sweeping changes in American education, and varying economic conditions, today's practitioner must respond as a dynamic leader, planner, and manager.

This book of cases, with its emphasis on practical management, is designed for library media specialists in elementary, middle, and high school settings. The cases are broadly grouped along the guidelines suggested by *Information Power* (the standards issued by the American Association of School Librarians) and are then subdivided by type of media center. The resources found in the appendixes and bibliography support the concepts found in the cases and should be consulted when formulating policies.

Whether you work in a rural high school or an urban elementary school, whether you have a fixed or flexible schedule, and whether you have heterogeneous or homogeneous groupings, this work will offer you the opportunity to analyze a situation and develop your own promising practice or benchmark for total quality service.

Acknowledgments

Gratitude is due to the many school media specialists who gave us suggestions based upon their own experiences. They are too numerous to list individually, but we hope they will accept our heartfelt thanks when they read the book.

We must also mention our appreciation to our families, who encouraged our efforts and critiqued the studies. Their reality check was invaluable.

We hope the book will be of value to students and practitioners alike. We found it a challenging effort that expresses our philosophies of library management services. Librarians are known for sharing, and we believe this to be our contribution to the profession.

I

ELEMENTARY SCHOOL LIBRARY MEDIA CENTERS

1

Leadership, Planning, and Management

1.1. Fixed, Flexible, Research Time: It's All in the Terminology

Anna West has been the library media specialist at the Horizons School for five years. Each of the six hundred Horizons students comes to the library media center once a week for forty-five minutes of instruction and book selection. Rarely do teachers come into the library media center. Generally, they drop off their students on their way to a meeting or the teachers' room for their preparation period. Anna is not particularly aggressive about drawing teachers in. She is very unassuming and prefers to work behind the scenes. She has become friendly with some teachers who have become active users of the library media center. Through their lunch conversations, Anna has become aware of their curriculum needs and has filled the void and then some. They cannot imagine not having her and her collection to back up their classroom presentations.

Anna has worked very hard building the collection at Horizons. She has used local funds, won numerous competitive grants, been the beneficiary of Parent Teacher Organization (PTO) fund-raisers, and held book fairs in the library. The collection is up to date and contains approximately 8,500 volumes. Anna's colleagues in Presto City respect her knowledge of her students and of the city's curriculum at the elementary level. Anna, however, is largely unrecognized in her own building. The teachers take for granted that she will be there and take their classes. They also take for granted the quality and quantity of the collection and Anna's willingness to go the extra mile to meet their information needs.

Anna is tired of being taken for granted and wants to break the pattern she has been in at Horizons. Anna went back to school this summer and learned about "flexible" scheduling. She is fascinated by the concept of resource-based instruction. Her fixed schedule of classes emphasizing card catalog or encyclopedia skills seems like something from the era of Melvil Dewey.

In August Anna makes an appointment to see the principal about her schedule. Her goal is to move from the present fixed schedule to one of complete flexibility. She points out to Principal Robrillo that she sees the children at Horizons fifteen minutes more per week than any other elementary library media specialist. She would like to put her classes on a thirty-minute time period and use the extra fifteen minutes from each class to create "research time." She would like to have the fifteen minutes gathered in blocks at either the beginning or end of each day. Since she normally has six forty-five minute classes each day, she will save ninety minutes per day for research. She assures him that she will still teach skills, allow for book selection, and cover the teachers' preparation periods.

Anna explains the concept of research time to the principal as a time when she will be in the library media center and the center will be open. During this time students may come in as individual users or in small groups, or teachers may schedule an entire class into the center. When a teacher brings a class, both Anna and that teacher will present the lesson. In some cases Anna will go into the classroom during that time to teach cooperatively with a teacher who will later bring her students into the center. Anna further points out to Mr. Robrillo that this is not a time for circulation—that will continue to occur during the class's regular library time.

The collection at Horizons is strong and should be able to support any research topic. Anna has been mapping the collection for years and knows not only the curriculum but the available literature. She has a wide collection of nonprint audiovisual sources that will add dimension to research projects. The principal is not convinced. He is a traditionalist who is not much of a library user himself. Out of respect for Anna, however, he doesn't say no. He tells her to put her plan in writing and be prepared to present it to the faculty. If they agree, then he will modify her schedule to allow for implementation of this "research time" beginning with the opening of school.

Questions

1. What should Anna put in writing about her new idea?
2. Is there anything wrong with what Anna has been doing for the last five years?
3. If Anna wants a flexible schedule, why doesn't just she ask for it?
4. How will Anna be able to do in thirty-minute time periods what she's been doing for years in forty-five-minute ones?
5. What is resource-based instruction and how does the library schedule get involved?
6. Are resource-based instruction and a fixed schedule completely incompatible?
7. How can Anna show that more readers will be served more effectively under the new plan?
8. What will Anna do to "market" this new research time?
9. How will the faculty feel about having fifteen minutes less free time?
10. Are there contract issues involved here?

1.2. Library Research for Kindergarten Students

Teachers at the King Elementary School are very concerned about the contract language and their allotted free or unassigned periods. The school's library media specialist is one of the people responsible, contractually, for covering the free or unassigned periods for classroom teachers. As a result, she has a very fixed schedule of library skills classes each day. During these fixed classes, in addition to teaching skills, she also does circulation, book talks, and storytelling. Further, the school library media specialist at King also has time each day called "open library." She has no bus or lunch monitoring duties and is given this time in her schedule to allow small groups of users to have open access to the library media center to do research, borrow and return books, and so on.

Janet Vasquez, the library media specialist at King, is very good about using this open-library time effectively and efficiently. She publicizes it well in advance each month and never misses an opportunity to talk with classroom teachers about sending their students to the library for research. There is one open-library period per day, generally of a forty-five-minute duration. The times are scattered throughout the days of the week so that as many teachers as possible may take advantage of this program.

Most teachers at King get a forty-five-minute unassigned or free period each day; this is in addition to a thirty-minute duty-free lunch. The kindergarten teacher, however, feels that she should get more because her students, by their very nature, are more demanding. She and the principal have had numerous confrontations about this subject and the kindergarten teacher, Ms. Mayfield, has filed several grievances about what she feels is an inequity. She has lost the grievances and the principal now refuses to discuss the situation with her.

This month when Ms. Vasquez sends out her sign-up sheet of open-library times, Ms. Mayfield signs up kindergarten children for each available period. The open-library guidelines say that no more than three or four students per classroom should be sent for open library at one time. Ms. Vasquez is very flexible with this and in general teachers respect the guidelines and work with her when special situations arise. The form for signing up asks the name and homeroom of the child as well as the date and time when the child is coming. The form also asks what the child will be working on—in other words, what research topic. Generally, Ms. Vasquez receives notice from the classroom teachers as new themes or strands are being presented. In the form completed by Ms. Mayfield she has indicated that the research topic is dinosaurs. She has signed up three students per day for each day during the month.

Ms. Vasquez is confused when the sign-up sheet returns to her. Most of the children who come to do research are second graders or above. Although sometimes in the spring first graders will be signed up, she has never had kindergarten students come for open library. Since the school department policy does not permit circulation of library materials to kindergartners, their fixed-schedule library time is devoted to a story and a related activity. Ms. Vasquez knows that dinosaurs are not part of the kindergarten curriculum and wonders what they will be doing during the open-library time. She feels that she is being used to babysit for Ms. Mayfield's students and is providing this classroom teacher with a reduced class load each day during the month. She also notices on the sign-up sheet that teachers that normally sign up have not. She is curious as to whether some larger issue is at play here. Is she going to be drawn into the issue of extra free periods for the kindergarten teacher?

Questions

1. How should Ms. Vasquez handle this situation?
2. Should she talk with the principal first?
3. Should she just agree to this situation for the month?
4. Can kindergarten children do research?
5. Should Ms. Vasquez set up a cooperative research assignment with Ms. Mayfield that would allow her students to come during open library but with a meaningful assignment that Ms. Vasquez is involved with?
6. How contentious should this situation be?
7. Doesn't the library media specialist have contract rights as well?
8. If class size is limited to twenty-six students and the open-library time often goes beyond this, how should she handle the situation?

1.3. Identifying and Responding to Teachers' Needs

Savann Soam has just transferred to the St. James Elementary School as the school library media specialist. Savann is a fairly new employee in the diocese of Waverly and is, in fact, new to the library profession and to the classroom. While in library school Savann focused on school librarianship with additional course work in technical services. Savann is well read in the areas of children's literature and school library media center management. She is eager to begin her responsibilities at St. James and comes in during August to get things organized. St. James has had several library media specialists over the last few years—none have stayed very long but no one is quite sure why. The collection is up to date and there are computers for CDs but no on-line catalog. There is an active PTO that is very supportive of the library media center and the principal, Brother Finian, is also a major supporter.

The weeks before school begins, Savann prepares the collection by checking shelf order and making signs. She hangs colorful posters promoting reading and checks out the vertical file and the CDs. While working away, she meets several of the teachers. They are most friendly and

Savann feels very welcome. She talks with them about what they will be teaching at the beginning of the school year and offers suggestions on incorporating some new picture books, some award winners, and some great nonfiction series into their classes. They assure her that once things are under way, they'll be back.

The library media center at St. James serves about eight hundred students in grades K–6. The center is flexibly scheduled and heavily used, according to annual reports that Savann finds in the files. The school is divided into two areas: primary, serving K–3, and intermediate, serving grades 4–6. There are approximately seventy teachers, mostly full-timers. There is a Library Committee made up of one special needs teacher, one reading resource teacher, and one teacher from both the primary and intermediate areas. The committee meets monthly to "advise" the library media specialist on book selection, curriculum issues, fund-raising, and so on. The principal chairs the meeting and is a voting member of the committee.

School starts off smoothly and Savann is busy checking out books to the children, who seem eager to come to the library media center. She posts a schedule of story hours and themes that the stories will focus on during the first quarter. Teachers from the primary area sign up to bring the children to most of the story times. Savann also sends around a notice about book talks for the older students. The teachers from the intermediate area tell her they are not ready yet to work with her on this but continue to send in students in small groups to the library media center to borrow books. Students also come during their lunch periods and before and after school to borrow books. The circulation is indeed quite impressive, as the back files have indicated. The materials that circulate are both fiction and nonfiction.

The first meeting of the Library Committee is held during the second week of school. Mostly it is social, with some updates on a new emphasis in the third-grade reading program. Savann makes a note to talk with the third-grade teachers. The October meeting focuses on fund-raising and how to increase attendance at the fund-raiser.

Savann is concerned about the way the library is perceived by the faculty. They are very friendly but not at all knowledgeable about children's literature and how to best incorporate it into the classroom. Savann, in her naiveté, hoped that the Library Committee would help her respond to the lack of connection between the library media center and the classroom. Clearly, as she's seen at the first two monthly meetings, they are not going to get involved with her concern in this matter. She is troubled because all she seems to do is tell a few stories and check out books. She has a vision of the library media center as the hub of the learning activities of the school. Instead, after two months she feels that she is not even an extension of the classroom but rather the keeper of the book room.

Savann is unsure of how to proceed. Should she talk with Brother Finian or some of the intermediate teachers? Should she talk with people at her library school? She has very little idea of what goes on in the intermediate classrooms at St. James—their curriculum, the teaching styles used, and the classroom management style and philosophy. She feels that the teachers don't see her at the hub but instead off to the side in a clerical rather than professional capacity. The *Information Power* guidelines see Savann as an instructional consultant, teacher, and information specialist. Not wishing to jeopardize the friendly atmosphere she has encountered, where does she go with her vision?

Questions

1. Whose vision is it that the library media center be the hub of learning activities for a school? Do the teachers believe this?
2. How can Savann convince them of the value of her services?
3. Should she deluge them with data or try to work directly with the principal?
4. Is there a way for Savann to work successfully with a small group of intermediate teachers in a pilot program?
5. If the faculty and principal see the library media specialist as keeper of the book room, is this why the position has had considerable turnover?
6. What kinds of records in the circulation back file would indicate that the library media center is heavily used? Is use defined as circulation only? Does use reflect a combination of storytelling and circulation?
7. How can Savann move her colleagues forward on this issue? How should she lead—by example; by statistics and charts; by bringing in other library media specialists who are moving their programs forward?

1.4. Reaching Out from the Shelves: Marketing the Library Media Center and Its Services

Julius Durrell has inherited a school library media center with no card catalog, about one thousand books in cartons, ten shelf units, a large room with windows and plenty of sun, and twenty-five little chairs for students. He has no idea where to begin. Julius is the first library media specialist based at the Primary School. The Primary School has been created due to overcrowding in the Holland Elementary School. All of the kindergarten and first grades have been transferred to the Primary School and Julius is there two days each week. The other three days, Julius serves as the second library media specialist at the bigger Holland School.

What Julius lacks in experience he makes up for in enthusiasm. His high energy level secured him this position. He came in every day for the two weeks before school started and unpacked the books, put them on the shelf, hung up posters, and organized his lessons. The students Julius sees at the Primary School come for thirty-minute periods either on Tuesday or Wednesday, the two days he is assigned there. In addition to his teaching responsibilities, Julius has lunch duty for thirty minutes each of those two days and an "open access" period each day. During the open-access time, Julius is in the library and small groups of students may come in independently to borrow materials or to research a specific topic.

The library media center is clean and obviously in some order. Without a card catalog or shelf list, however, Julius has no idea what he owns and where there are gaps in the collection. Julius wants to be an asset to the Primary School and surveys the teachers about their needs. From their input he searches his existing collection, identifies materials to purchase, and generates a purchase order. The new materials arrive by Thanksgiving. While waiting for the new materials to arrive, Julius begins to catalog the backlog. He gets money from the PTO to purchase catalog cards from a company that provides a complete set of cards, pockets and pocket cards, bar-code and MicroLif data. Someday, Julius knows they'll automate all of the libraries in his rural area. Julius puts the books on the shelves, files the cards in a card file, and notifies the teachers of the availability of the new resources.

During the first few weeks everyone stops by to see the "real" library. Some teachers who have never borrowed materials begin to do so. After Christmas, however, things die down and Julius seems to be back in his role of covering classes. The open-access time is rarely used except by the occasional student who wants to renew a book. Julius begins to feel discouraged by the lack of circulation and overall use of the library. He talks to a friend about it one night and his friend suggests that Julius develop a plan to market his library to the faculty and administration at the Primary School. Julius thinks that this is just too businesslike but he begins to search the literature for ways to go about improving the perception of his role and that of the library media center.

What Julius finds absolutely amazes him. He begins by searching in various periodical indexes and then asks colleagues on LM_NET (a library media Internet e-mail system) about his problem. He gets lots of citations and lots of advice. Basically, he realizes that he has a viable product to sell—one that teachers will buy and students will use. Further, he realizes that the parents and his community could be involved actively as fund-raisers, readers, volunteers, and so on. His job is to make sure that his product is useful and current. How he does this and how that strategy is assessed or evaluated is his task. Julius finds himself renewed and begins to develop a marketing plan.

Questions

1. How should Julius begin? With a needs assessment or market analysis? What exactly is a needs assessment or market analysis and whose needs/market would Julius be assessing?
2. Is there a place in the school library media field for using such business tools as a market analysis?
3. What if people really want more than Julius can possibly deliver in his two days at the Primary School?
4. Should Julius focus on one small issue like support for a particular thematic unit or the need to develop a professional collection for teachers? He could then come up with a solution, try it, refine it, and implement it. Then he could go on to other issues like why he is only at the Primary School two days a week.

2
Personnel

2.1. Decisions, Decisions, Decisions. What to Do about a Job?

Katie West has been a librarian for twenty-two years. She has worked in public, academic, and special libraries. During her years as a librarian, she has earned several graduate degrees—one in business, one in history—and is now working on one in computer applications. As an undergraduate, Katie majored in history but also earned certification as an elementary school teacher. She went right to library school and has never taught. Her certification in elementary education is for life, however, as that was what her state gave upon completion of student teaching. Katie has been married for eighteen years to Tom, an industrial engineer. Tom works for a large manufacturer and has been transferred several times during their marriage.

Last month, Tom was offered a major promotion and after discussing the position with Katie, he decided to accept it. The position requires him to relocate to Capital City within the next few weeks. Katie stays behind and sells the house. About six months after the move Katie joins Tom in their new house.

Katie begins to job search and sends out resumes. She goes on several interviews but just isn't excited about the positions. Katie has job-hopped because of Tom and now realizes that pension benefits and job security are becoming more important to her as she heads into her fifties.

One night, Katie talks with her neighbor Bertha, who works for the Capital City School Department as a secretary. She says that they are always looking for teachers and encourages Katie to sign up to substitute.

Katie does not want to substitute but thinks that maybe teaching business or computers in a high school might be fun.

On Thursday morning Katie goes to the Capital City School Department and submits an application along with her resume. She also submits a photocopy of her lifetime certification and photocopies of her transcripts. Three days later, Katie receives a call from Georgia Easton, a school department recruiter, to come in for an interview the next day.

Katie knows little or nothing about the Capital City School Department, other than what she hears from her neighbors and their children. Capital City is the largest city in the state and has over 26,000 students in about 50 schools. The population is diverse and the funding is small. Katie decides that she'll just go into the interview cold and take her cues about the district from Ms. Easton. She does read the newspapers that have come into the house in the last few days and focuses on the news about the schools. From the papers she learns that even though it is January, there are many positions that are filled with substitutes because there just are no certified people in those disciplines. Katie learns to her surprise that nine of the schools have no library media specialist.

At the interview Ms. Easton simply verifies what Katie has in her resume—that she has a master of library science degree, is a city resident (there is a residency requirement), and has an elementary certification from another state. Ms. Easton then takes Katie to meet Jorge Ramos, the school library media supervisor. Mr. Ramos is working in his office and clearly knows nothing about Katie's application. He seems surprised when Ms. Easton introduces them. He asks Katie if the address on her resume is a permanent one and if she has completed her MLS. Katie responds affirmatively to both questions and is clearly puzzled. Mr. Ramos then leans back in his chair, points to a map of the city, and tells Katie to pick a school she'd like to work in; she can start in the morning.

Katie is flabbergasted and asks Mr. Ramos to tell her something about the schools. As he talks, she begins to focus on the type of position she would like—a single school so that she wouldn't have to travel; a diverse population but not too large; and a stable faculty. Mr. Ramos begins to tell Katie about the Mallyn Elementary School. He talks and she listens. At the end of forty-five minutes, Katie says she would like to see the school and meet with the principal. Mr. Ramos says that is not possible as time is of the essence. If she wants the job, she should say yes now; she can always transfer at the end of the term. Since she already has an elementary certificate, she is eligible for emergency certification. The job is hers, Mr. Ramos says, strike while the iron is hot.

Katie realizes that Capital, compensating her for all of her years of experience, will start her at $48,000. She will have free health coverage and will only work 180 days. She'll have the summer off and will only need to take three graduate courses to get certified as a school library media specialist. She quickly makes a decision and tells Mr. Ramos.

Questions

1. Does Katie want to be a school library media specialist? Has she done any serious thinking about it?
2. How does the position of school library media specialist differ from that of the classroom teacher?
3. How is the role of the school library media specialist different than or the same as the types of positions Katie's held in her career?
4. Does Katie have a real sense of what she's getting into?
5. Why is Katie not permitted to visit Mallyn and how should she handle this? Have Katie's varied experiences prepared her for this new position?
6. What is the role of Ms. Easton, the recruiter? What is the personnel role of Mr. Ramos, the school library media supervisor?
7. Katie met with the recruiter and was then offered the position at Mallyn by the school library media supervisor. What does this say about personnel hiring practices in Capital City?

2.2. Whose Library Media Center Is It? Who's in Charge?

The state standards for school library media centers say that when a school reaches an enrollment of 500 students, there must be one full-time library media specialist assigned to the building on a full-time basis. The standards were written in 1966 and have not been updated. There is no provision in place for when a school reaches 800 or 900 students, but past practice allows for one additional library media specialist when 900 students are enrolled in the same building.

Alex Southern is the full-time library media specialist at the Western

Junction Elementary School. He has been at Western for nine years. Alex is the consummate professional—runs a superb program on a fixed schedule, opens the library before hours, works cooperatively with teachers on his free period, is active in the PTO, and sits on the school management team. Alex is highly respected by students and peers alike. He has turned the library media center around from a "book storehouse" to the hub of the school. Although funding has been tight, he has been most creative and successful in writing grants, holding book fairs, and even winning prizes at the American Library Association (ALA) and the American Association of School Librarians (AASL) conventions.

The enrollment at Western is 980 students in grades K–6 and today is the first day of school. Alex knows from past experiences that at least twenty more students will enroll during the first week. Western is in a rapidly growing section of the city and offers several specialized programs including full-day kindergarten, bilingual Spanish, and an inclusion model for special education instruction that is the model for the state.

Because there is a shortage of school library media specialists, the second library staff member at Western has been a certified classroom teacher who takes the job at Western at substitute pay. This person subs until a classroom opens up. When that happens, the sub in the library leaves and another takes over. In the last few years Alex has had as many as four different people working as subs per year in that second position. None of the subs has a master of library science degree (MLS), and even though Alex tries hard to talk with them about making the job permanent once half of the MLS is completed, none picks this career.

Alex is assigned to the library media center with fixed-schedule classes three days per week; Thursday and Friday are open so that teachers and small groups of students may come in for research. Alex does his most creative resource-based instruction on these two days. By his own admission, these days keep him sane and, he hopes, are laying the groundwork for a more flexible schedule in the future. The substitute library media specialist is assigned to Western on Thursdays and Fridays and holds classes in the classroom. Circulation does not take place and only skills are taught. Because of the nature of the position and the person filling it, Alex writes the lesson plans and sets policy for the classes that the sub covers.

Paco Rodriguez is the new substitute teacher assigned to cover Thursdays and Fridays at Western. A recent graduate of the university, Paco has never taught before but is very enthusiastic. His major was elementary education, but he worked his way through school by working as a shelver in the university's curriculum library. There, he got to know the children's literature collection. He is an avid reader and has a flair for art. He is very enthusiastic after being assigned to Western. He is optimistic that he'll get a program going there that combines art and children's literature. Paco is simply told by the hiring office to report at 9 A.M. on September 1. He is told that he will only be at Western for two days a week and that a placement will be found for him for the other days.

Paco shows up at Western and is startled to find out that he is the second library media specialist. He is confused because he feels that although he's only a sub, he should be permitted to bring his classes to the library media center. He finds Alex to be friendly but firm on this issue. Together they work on what kinds of skills will be taught and how they'll be taught. Alex takes Paco around to meet the teachers whose classes he will be teaching and to show him where supplies and the like are kept. The two men get along just fine, but Paco is uneasy about the job. He wonders whether or not this is really the place for him. There seems to be little room for creativity and no chance to work on projects with teachers.

Alex also is uneasy. Something about Paco seems to set him apart from the other subs; perhaps it is his knowledge of children's literature or his talk about art integration. Alex thinks that this may be the sub he can convince to go earn an MLS. Meanwhile, he's had the revolving door of subs and so Paco will just have to follow the procedures that Alex has established.

Questions

1. Is Alex really the supervisor in this situation? Should he be since he has the certification, the knowledge, and the responsibility and is based permanently at Western Junction?
2. Is Alex depriving a percentage of the students at Western Junction (perhaps as much as 40 percent) of the opportunity to learn about the library media center in the center itself?
3. Do classroom teachers have a right to expect that their students will have library class in the library media center?
4. What gives Alex the right to decide what and how Paco teaches his class?
5. What role does the principal have in all of this? How about the role of the supervisor of library media services for the district?

6. Do you think that the office that assigned Paco to this placement is aware of what he's to do?
7. How should Paco proceed if he wants to change this situation?
8. If Paco was permanent at Western Junction and had an MLS, how could this work out?
9. What incentives are there for Paco or anyone to get an MLS in order to be the second library media specialist (closed out of the library media center) at a large school like this?

2.3. Getting Out—Transfer Solves a Difficult Situation

The Hamilton Avenue School has long been regarded as out of sync with reform efforts in the city of Pennsville. The principal has been there for several years and made no effort to move the school toward site-based management, resource-based instruction, and the like. The teachers teach individually, not in teams, and the library media center harkens back to the 1960s in both physical appearance and collection. The library media specialist, Marcello Barros, has been at Hamilton Avenue for nearly fifteen years. His efforts at Hamilton have been largely confined to getting through the grueling schedule of fixed classes for nearly 850 students in grades K–6. He has no time in his schedule for collection development, working with teachers, writing grants, and so on. Technology in his whole school is nonexistent so he makes no effort to secure hardware and software for the library media center.

In 1995, the city of Pennsville was chosen by the Westingly Foundation as the recipient of a $1.2 million grant for improving library services for at-risk children. Each of the thirty or so schools serving children in grades K–8 was eligible for money for physical renovation, programming, and collection development. The catch for receiving this money, however, was demonstration of reform efforts in school management (councils with decision makers drawn from parents, teachers, and the community) and a move toward resource-based instruction. Each school had to write a grant explaining how they would move forward in these directions. The grant had to be written by a team consisting of the library media specialist, the principal, parents, and teachers. Money was also available for training in team dynamics and grant writing. Two summer institutes were offered in program planning and implementation and use of on-line resources.

Marcello and his school principal, Samantha Gerston, were involved in the early stages of applying for the Westingly grant. They planned for renovation of the library media center and worked cooperatively on a planning team with parents to identify gaps in the collection. The team came up with a plan to move toward resource-based instruction by focusing on thematic units. Samantha, however, was not interested in other than cursory planning for the development and future implementation of a school improvement plan. Their school grant application reflected a slight shift toward the site-based management asked for in the grant, but only that. The Hamilton Avenue School received the grant money and began to implement the changes identified. The changes in the physical plant and the collection were so startling that people in the community began to take notice.

As the grant process continued, lots of positive press ensued. Samantha and Marcello went to regional and national conferences talking about their innovative partnership. Samantha seemed converted to the concept of resource-based instruction and was viewed in the city as a beacon of hope for the thirty-plus fixed-schedule school library media specialists. The grant continued for three years and each year Samantha was held up as a model of an enlightened principal. Marcello's fixed schedule remained the same, however, although lunch and bus duty were taken away and that time was classified as library research time. During these periods, Marcello was available for small group instruction, special projects, and the like. True, there were some new books along with tables and chairs and a rug, but it really seemed like so much smoke and mirrors. Any move toward a flexible schedule was thwarted and teachers met in teams without him or his input. Themes were developed without regard to library resources.

In September, Hamilton Avenue School, along with the rest of Pennsville, experienced a tremendous growth in enrollment. Overcrowding was the norm. Samantha converted the library media center to a classroom and forced Marcello to hold his classes in the students' homerooms. Samantha never talked with Marcello about the situation or how long it would last and what other alternatives were available. Marcello tried to speak with Samantha but she was always busy with parents, and bus and student schedules. Back was lunch and bus duty for Marcello and gone was library research time. The card catalog was used as a piece of furniture; the books were taken off the shelf and stored by the custodians.

Over Columbus Day weekend Marcello thought about his options. When school opened the next Tuesday, he went to the Human Resources Department and filed a transfer request. He told no one about this and continued to function at Hamilton Avenue on a rolling cart. There was no circulation, just skills, taught in isolation, and lunch and bus duty.

On February 1, Marcello accepted a transfer and began work the next week. His fifteen years at Hamilton ended without a word of thanks from Samantha. He packed up his personal items and began anew in a building that had a mixture of fixed and flexible scheduling, an active site team, and a long-range plan implementing technology.

Questions

1. Since the school grant reflected only a slight shift toward site-based management, should the Westingly Foundation have funded it?
2. If this was a three-year proposal were there checks and balances for Westingly to monitor the movement forward at each stage of the grant?
3. Was Samantha justified in using the library media center for a classroom?
4. What professional responsibility does Marcello have to begin a dialog with Samantha before transferring out? Did either party learn from this experience?
5. Should the grant administrator have monitored more closely what was going on at Hamilton Avenue?
6. Is there an accountability issue here?
7. What kind of professional policy could have been implemented to allow Marcello to voice a complaint about being displaced?
8. What role does the school library media district supervisor play in this situation?

2.4. The Take-Charge Clerk and the Timid Library Media Specialist

St. Briget's School is located in the heart of the most rural part of the tri-state area. Founded in 1880, it is the oldest school in continuous operation in the region. Nearly eight hundred students attend classes there in grades K–8. The school is staffed primarily by the Sisters of Religion but there are lay teachers in some positions. One of the positions is a clerical one staffed by Debby Minton. Debby is a graduate of St. Briget's and returned to the area after many years away. She is the divorced mother of four. Debby has a high school diploma and little work experience. She has been in the front office answering the phone and doing some light typing for about a semester. She is very much a take-charge–type person, even when she is not responsible for a particular area. She considers herself equal to any of the teaching staff and will often intervene when a parent and teacher are discussing an issue. She often takes over from the school secretary and advises parents on school policy. Many times she seems to step on people's toes, parents and staff alike. No one says anything to her in these situations because the principal seems to like her and they often have lunch together.

Bhun Phong is another lay instructor. She is the school library media specialist. Bhun has a master of library science degree (MLS) from the local university and has worked for many years in a variety of types of libraries around the world. Her knowledge base is strong but her English is heavily accented. Because of this, she is often reticent when she should be in control of an issue. She is well liked by the students and has a warmth about her that causes people to respond to her in a kindly manner.

Sister Ignatius, the principal, has come to Bhun with a problem. Debby has ruffled quite a few feathers in the front office, and while this is not cause for dismissal, she clearly cannot remain there. Sister likes Debby personally but knows that the image of St. Briget's is being affected by Debby's behavior. Debby is a hard worker but likes to worry about things beyond her responsibility. Sister hopes that by placing Debby in the library media center, some awkwardness may be diffused. Since Bhun has recently begun to automate the library media center, and made a strong case for clerical support, Sister thinks that this transfer will kill two birds with one stone.

Bhun is most grateful for the assistance, although she is rather intimidated by Debby. She consoles herself with the thought that she knows much more than Debby about libraries and computerization. Sister says that she will take care of presenting the transfer to Debby in the best possible light. Debby is to start in two weeks.

True to her word, Sister Ignatius presents the clerical position in the library media center to Debby in such a way that she is thrilled. The transfer, she tells people, is because Bhun is having difficulty in the library media center and she (Debby) has such good office skills that Sister literally had to beg her to help out. Debby embellishes the transfer with each telling. Bhun, of course, hears what Debby is saying, but true to her behavior, says nothing to countermand it.

On the day that Debby is to transfer to the school's library media center, Bhun stops on her way to work to pick up a plant and some bagels. Bhun wants to start off on the right foot with Debby. In spite of her brashness, Debby is a hard worker and will, Bhun feels, with training make a substantial contribution to the smooth running of the new automated systems. When Bhun arrives for work, she is about a half an hour earlier than normal. When she walks into her office, Debby is sitting at her desk talking on the phone. Bhun hangs up her coat and puts the bagels on a tray and prepares some coffee. Debby continues what is obviously a personal phone call. Bhun leaves the office and begins to turn on the lights in the reading room, puts out the day's newspapers, and looks about the room. She sips some coffee and waits—growing more angry as the time passes. About ten minutes later, Debby comes out into the reading room, coffee and bagel in hand, and says, "Well, let's get started here. Sister Ignatius says you're in tough shape and I'm here to solve your problems." Bhun looks at Debby, smiles, and begins to talk with her about the automating project.

Questions

1. Why did the principal choose placing Debby into the library media center as the solution to her personnel problem? Why was the media center the best out?
2. How should she and Bhun have best outlined supervision of Debby, Debby's responsibilities, and Debby's overall role in the library media center?

3. How can Bhun counter Debby's perception of her transfer to the library media center? Should she?
4. Should Bhun establish the ground rules of the workday right away?
5. Is Bhun better off having no clerical assistance than one with this type of dominant personality?

3
Resources and Equipment

3.1. Alternative Professional Collection

The Potterville Elementary School has long been on the forefront of educational change. Established in the early 1960s as an alternative to busing, Potterville offers special emphasis in science and math as well as a full-time social worker, nurse practitioner, and enrichment programs before and after school. Parents sign up to send their children on lengthy bus rides just to take advantage of Potterville's programs.

Two years ago Potterville beat out 135 other elementary schools in the state and was awarded the coveted title of "Red Ribbon School." With this title came about $250,000 in state monies to create a model for schools of the future. Building on an already strong base, the Grant Committee (consisting of the library media specialist; the building delegate, who is also a sixth-grade teacher; and third-grade, fourth-grade, and fifth-grade classroom teachers) proposed academic changes as well as changes in the governance of the school. The library media specialist was very involved in the writing of the academic portion of the grant as she holds not only a master of library science (MLS) but a master of arts in teaching (MAT). She has written curriculum for other school districts and teaches at the local college. The fifth- and sixth-grade teachers focused exclusively on the governance portion of the grant.

The road to school change is often rocky, and the experiences at Potterville are no exception. The Grant Committee does not always see eye to eye on the implementation of the programs. Nonetheless, they realize that they are breaking new ground and try not to let the situation get the better of them, either personally or professionally.

One portion of the governance side of the grant speaks to the development of a professional collection of resources. The fifth- and sixth-grade teachers who authored this portion had in mind a collection of print and nonprint resources that would allow teachers to see promising practices of school reform, be they curriculum related, governance related, or so on. These two teachers see the governance and the academic portions of school restructuring as intertwined. Without consulting with the library media specialist they order materials through the local bookstore.

The library media center at Potterville has about nine thousand volumes and serves a student population of seven hundred students. Over the years the library media specialist has developed a collection of materials in support of the curriculum. These are widely used, and she continues to develop this portion of the collection. When she speaks to the members of the Grant Committee about using the Red Ribbon School funds to add to this existing collection they indicate that their vision is to create a new collection and house it in the teachers' room. There, located next to the copier, the fax, and a telephone, they feel it will be better utilized. They want to keep the materials uncataloged so that teachers will not be intimidated by library-type borrowing procedures.

The library media specialist is livid. She has been tip-toeing around the teachers on the Grant Committee for far too long. She has single-handedly written that portion of the Red Ribbon Grant that she feels will have the most lasting impact—the academic portion. She feels betrayed and strikes out with the only weapon she has—the pen. In an open letter to the faculty she presents the historical background on the grant and the library media center. She stresses the connection between academic and governance issues. She informs the faculty that unless the new acquisitions to the Professional Collection are cataloged and housed in the library media center with the existing materials, the monies will be wasted, the new titles underutilized, and many even lost. Time will be wasted as teachers struggle to find items of interest and try remembering what they've seen in the collection. She points out that by cataloging the materials into the on-line catalog, greater accessibility will be assured.

Questions

1. What is wrong with the Grant Committee's proposal?
2. What problem is created by ordering materials for a separate collection from a local bookstore?

3. Library circulation procedures are often intimidating, so why not just put these materials out in a less-structured atmosphere and let these teachers be responsible?
4. These materials are not really the responsibility of the library media specialist, so why is she so concerned?
5. What's the conflict about specialized, uncataloged collections that are used by the teachers?
6. Is there a middle road on this issue?
7. May the materials be acquired and cataloged but housed in a separate place?

3.2. Whole Language versus Phonics Resources

The Michelson School District has no formal policy nor any type of guidelines for teaching reading. They have suggested a reading textbook series that covers grades K–8 but leaves the actual implementation of skills and adoption of the text up to the local school's administration. While the controversy regarding whole language versus phonics shakes the very foundation of the reading profession, Michelson is oblivious.

Largo Heights Elementary is one of the larger schools in the district. Approximately eight hundred students in grades K–5 attend there. In addition, there are three self-contained special education rooms as well as three bilingual Spanish classes. Jerry Veira, the library media specialist, has been at the school for about eight years. He is a well-respected member of the faculty, known for his humor as well as his attention to detail. Because of his flexible schedule, Jerry has plenty of opportunity to work with all of the faculty and students. His wise use of time and ability to handle many demanding activities at one time has resulted in a viable center.

The library media center budget in Largo Heights is split into two sections: primary and intermediate resources. Since the enrollment in the primary grades (defined as kindergarten through grade 2) is approximately the same as that for intermediate (grades 3–5), the funds are split rather evenly. For the last five years Jerry has spent the bulk of the primary monies on materials that support several literacy themes used by two primary teachers. These teachers work in conjunction with one another and Jerry feels that they are very forward-thinking. They share their information, themes, and the like with the other primary-grade teachers with some success. As a whole, though, each of the kindergarten through grade 2 teachers handles reading in his or her own way, not necessarily consistent across grade levels.

This year, a new teacher transferred to Largo Heights. Maggie Acorn is an experienced second-grade teacher who believes phonics is the only way to teach reading. She bases this belief on her years in the classroom, not only in the Michelson School District but in other communities as well. She feels strongly that the district should make a decision regarding reading instruction, and that decision should reflect an emphasis on phonics. Maggie is an avid library user and makes an appointment to meet with Jerry during one of their common planning times.

At this meeting, Maggie tells Jerry she is impressed with the layout of the library media center and with its reputation throughout the system. She discusses a schedule with Jerry to bring her classes in to work on selecting a reading book that is age and interest appropriate. Maggie also wants the book they select to be one that they can and will read. She is concerned about the abundance of picture books in the library media center. She is familiar with them and comments on their high reading level—designed to be read to second graders rather than by them. Jerry tells her that they were bought in support of some themes. Maggie tells Jerry that she wants trade books that will allow for the several reading levels in her room and suggests several series that are available. Jerry tells her he will check on their availability and get back to her.

Jerry is in the process of putting together a book order for the next quarter and has already committed a sizeable portion of his primary-grade allocation to the themes adopted by the two teachers he works closely with. He had told them what he will be purchasing and is not sure that he can find additional monies for Maggie Acorn's suggested series. It is only September and he doesn't think Maggie's students are ready to actually take out books they can read, so maybe he can make do with the picture books for a while and later get her a few titles. She seems nice enough, but this is only her first month at Largo Heights and she may decide to get involved with the themes and whole-language approach that his friends use.

Questions

1. What should Jerry do about Maggie's request for books that her students "can and will read"?
2. Should he try to postpone buying anything until the next quarter and then buy something to appease her?
3. Should Jerry try to connect Maggie with his whole-language friends in hopes that they can reach a compromise agreement?
4. What obligation does Jerry have to support Maggie's request?
5. What about the other primary-grade teachers who don't seem to be represented?
6. Should Jerry do some collection mapping and then talk with all of the primary teachers before making any purchases?
7. What is the role here for the principal or the library media supervisor or even the reading supervisor?

3.3. How Many CD Workstations Are Enough?

Andres Pacheco is the library media specialist at the St. Vincent Elementary School. He is still working on his master of library science degree (MLS) but has over ten years of classroom teaching experience. He has been at St. Vincent's for about two years and is the school's first library media specialist. The school has always had a library media center, but generally it was staffed by parent volunteers. The collection does not yet meet Andres's expectations, so he is constantly meeting with teachers, mapping the collection, and buying for identified areas.

One area that is singularly lacking is that of technology. Andres is a real technology buff. He has an IBM Pentium at home and uses it for word processing, grades and registers, surfing the Internet, and running CD-ROMs. The library media center at St. Vincent has recently received two Macintosh 570s with CD-ROM drives. The computers have color monitors, and, although there is only one printer, Andres can't wait to get started using the new equipment. The machines came from a local cooperative grocery store that allowed their buyers to accumulate points for computer purchases. Andres made sure that the word got out and everyone sent in their grocery slips.

Although he's not too comfortable working with the Mac, Andres is sure that he will have no problem transferring his skills. He comes in on a few Saturdays and works on some of the software that came with the units. He then decides to buy an "elementary bundle" of software that he sees advertised in the Sunday paper. This bundle contains ten CDs, including an encyclopedia, a dictionary, and programs on animals, fish, sports, American history, world maps, Indians, Egypt, and the Middle Ages. He loads the CDs into the hard drive for ease of use and is ready to bring his students into the twenty-first century.

Andres decides to split the bundle and to put several of the CDs at one station and position that station at one end of the room. Also at that end are the nonfiction works and some tables for group work. The other half of the bundle goes to the Mac located at the opposite end of the room, where the picture books are located. After much thought, the printer goes in the center of the room, near his desk. Andres locates a small, cast-off TV cart and puts the printer on it. He loads the printer software into each computer so that all he has to do is wheel the printer over to the appropriate machine and connect it. He vows that his next purchase through the grocery receipts will be a second printer.

Now Andres is ready to show his students and faculty his new toy. He has a fixed schedule, so there is a limited amount of time each day to work with teachers and their classes. He does have one period per day, however, for these types of lessons and vows to use it wisely. During the first Monday that his machines are up and running, Andres has two second-grade classes and a fourth-grade class. He calls up the CD on animals at the station nearest the picture books. At the other station he sets up the CD on Indians. He plans to talk with the teachers about having their students come in independently to do research in these areas. For now, however, he just wants to show the students what the possibilities are. Andres has each group of children move their chairs in a semicircle around the computer. He introduces his lesson standing in front of the computer and then sits at the computer to do the demonstration. The children are straining to see the screen and much shoving and jockeying for position ensues. He walks them through several types of animals—pets, mammals, endangered species, and so on. The children all want a turn using the mouse and no one seems to be quiet enough to hear the sounds made by the animals. Andres keeps having to stop and draw the children back into the lesson. Even though he has few if any classroom-management problems, this day seems to bring out the worst in his students. The same type of behavior repeats itself during his other second-grade class, and during the fourth-grade class someone falls off their chair and gets hurt.

Andres is crushed. His new toy is not what he expected. How is he going to bring his students into the technology age with just two machines? The software installed on both hard drives includes a telecommunications package, and he had planned to teach his fifth-grade students how to search the Internet. He is disappointed and isn't sure that technology in the library media center is such a good idea. He vows to bring this problem up in the library class he is taking at the local university the next evening.

Questions

1. What is Andres's plan for using the technology in the library media center? How do the CD-ROMs fit into this?
2. Are second graders too young for this type of technology or software? What age level is best suited to using the new technology?
3. What can Andres do to maximize use of these two machines? Will hooking up the monitors to a TV help?
4. Should Andres have waited to introduce the technology to the students until he had more machines? If Andres is relying on grocery store receipts to bring in technology, how long will it take and what should he do in the meantime?
5. As this process continues, machines will be upgraded and he runs the risk of having ten or twelve different Macintoshes in the library media center. What should he do about this? How should he plan? Is this acceptable?
6. Do at least some of the students need some introduction to using the machines before using the software on CD? If so, how and where will they get this training?

3.4. Resources at Annex Facilities

The schools in the Catholic diocese of Stanton are bursting at the seams. Brother Finian Wise, the school superintendent, is worried. He looks at the enrollment for the coming school year and begins to call around to see about renting space. A recent census of the diocese indicates that enrollments will continue to rise about 4 percent per year for the next five years. The planning committee decides to add on annexes to three of the schools in the most densely populated parishes. At two of the schools, the annexes are in space rented and renovated by the diocese. At the third school, portable classrooms are used. Annex One at St. Brendan houses eight classrooms in a vacated YWCA. At St. Scholastica eight classrooms are placed in the old convent and gymnasium. At Holy Martyrs there are six classes in portable rooms in trailers. The portable rooms are brought in by truck but laid on a foundation. They are a type of prefab with brick put on the exterior at the scene.

The diocese spends all summer renovating the spaces. A giant public relations campaign is conducted in the three parishes to ensure that all understand that these annexes are not second-class classrooms. In fact, the opposite is true. With carpeting, new furniture, computers in every room, and air conditioning in the portable rooms, they are the envy of the teaching staff. The planning team for the diocese has decided to create primary schools in these annex classrooms and house only kindergarten and first grade there. The annexes then will ease overcrowding in the main buildings where the older children in grades two through eight will remain. The kindergarten teachers at all of the annexes will work together on selecting themes and texts. Each kindergarten will have a full-day schedule. The first-grade teachers at all annexes will likewise work together selecting books, thematic units, and the like. Two weeks has been set aside for summer curriculum writing by all first-grade and kindergarten teachers. Things seem ready to go.

On the first day of the summer curriculum writing session, Sister Ignatius asks about the organization of the day for the full-day kindergarten. She has been a kindergarten teacher for many years but always had half-day programs. She has been pushing for a full-day program for quite a while. While all of the teachers discuss their ideas, something is suddenly clear—there is no plan for library services. In the past at all three schools, each class had at least one period a week when they went to the library. The class activities varied and depended upon the ages of the children. The teachers and the library media specialist worked together to select materials to be read to the children and to have them borrow. They also developed a craft related to a story and so on. Somehow in all of the building plans, library services seems to have been overlooked. It is not possible for the library media specialist at each school to pick up eight additional classes; however, Sister Ignatius is most insistent that library services be provided. She feels strongly that if the students don't get into the "library habit" (her little joke) in the kindergarten and first-grade years, then they never will. The twenty-two kindergarten teachers listen to her and, because of her reputation, follow her lead in asking Brother Finian to secure space for library media centers in the annexes.

Brother Finian is willing to purchase materials for the kindergarten and first-grade annex classes, but he draws the line at creating a library media center. There is simply not any more money for space. He agrees to keep an open mind as Sister works with the three library media specialists to present some options for services that will not require a separate library media center. He is undecided about staffing but feels that the space issue must be settled first.

Sister Ignatius meets with the library media specialists from St. Brendan, St. Scholastica, and Holy Martyrs. Together they decide to spend about $10 per child for a start-up collection, focus on the themes selected for each grade level, have an on-line catalog, and use a laptop for circulation and searching. They decide to buy book trucks for holding big books; book trucks which have bins on the top for browsing as well as shelving space of a more traditional type at the bottom. This will serve as the portable library for all three annexes. Also slated to be purchased are several locked cabinets for nonprint resources and wall-mounted display cases that can be used to entice student use of the library media center. Armed with data, cost estimates, and a plan for hiring someone to be responsible for this portable library at each annex, the sister and her three colleagues make an appointment to see Brother Finian Wise.

Questions

1. Is this plan adequate for delivery of library services to a primary-school population?

2. Why don't the three library media specialists and Sister Ignatius go to the three parish administrators and insist upon creation of "mini" library media centers for these annex buildings?
3. Each of the annex buildings is close to the main school. Isn't it possible for the present library media specialists to adjust their schedules so that at least once in a while the children from the annexes can visit the main building's library media center?

4
Facilities

4.1. Forty Days and Forty Nights—Damage beyond Belief

Andy is the library media specialist for the Plainville Elementary School. This urban school has a population of about seven hundred students in grades K–5. The collection is good; in fact, some would say it was great. There are about 9,000 volumes, an on-line catalog, three computer stations, periodical subscriptions, and numerous CD-ROM software products. The downside is Andy's fixed schedule. The thirty classes Andy holds each week cover the teachers' free periods. Andy likes the kids and tries to get to know them—not an easy task with so many classes. He does plan his program well in advance, and he tells stories and circulates books each week to the students in grades K–2.

For students in grades 3–5, Andy does a combination of skills training (the on-line catalog, the periodical index, and the CD products) and book talks telling the students about good books to read. He has good attendance, is well prepared, and manages his classes appropriately, and the teachers love him. Andy knows, however, that his way of working is not current. There is no resource-based instruction or flexible schedule at Plainville. Andy's courses are taught in isolation from the classroom without any correlation to the curriculum. Andy doesn't want to be contentious, however, and feels the principal will tell him if resource-based instruction is necessary.

Andy has been at Plainville only two years. His predecessor was a real go-getter. She wrote grants, automated the collection, did planning with the classroom teachers, and so on. She was pushing for a flexible schedule when her husband was transferred. The teachers loved her too, although her style and Andy's differ considerably. Andy often refers to her as "super librarian." She moved away three years ago and for one year the library media center had a series of substitutes. Andy transferred from another elementary school because he felt that succeeding "super librarian" would be perfect—the place was in great shape and all the work was done. He only had to maintain what was there. The schedule didn't bother him. He did the job and went home at night and didn't even think about school.

This year Andy went away for several weeks at the beginning of the summer. When he got home, he found a message on his answering machine from Clement Washington, the principal at Plainville. The message was from the previous week and said that the roof had leaked at Plainville and there was some damage in the library. Andy called Clement, who played down the damage. Andy told Clement that he would visit the school during the coming week and examine the library media center. Three days later, Andy was allowed in the building. He opened the door to the center. The room smelled awful—a combination of mold and mildew. There was no water on the floor because the custodians had quickly mopped it up. There was not a lot of obvious damage, and Andy couldn't figure out the smell. He opened the windows and turned on the two window fans to pull the dank air out of the room. Then he went over to his desk, and that's when he saw it.

Everything that was uncovered in about a twelve-square-foot area had been soaked. The custodians had mopped up the water on the floor but had done nothing more. The floor tiles were coming up. New books had come in and were sitting in their shipping cartons near the windows. The cartons were unopened but appeared to have been water damaged. The picture books located near the windows also showed signs of water damage. The stuffed animals and puppets that Andy used to supplement his storytelling looked matted and felt damp. Andy didn't know what to do. He went to sit at his desk chair and even that upholstery was clammy. He stopped to think about his course of action.

Andy called two friends who worked at the university library in the Special Collections Department. Grace and Ed came over to see the damage later that day. They told Andy it was too late to do any kind of salvage work. They recommended a course of action that would proceed simultaneously in several directions. Andy needed to identify the damaged books and materials and then marshal the efforts of the custodial staff to remove them. Andy and the custodians, they said, should wear latex gloves and masks as protection from the mold and mildew. Next, they insisted that Andy meet with the principal as well as the library media supervisor. During this meeting Andy should impress upon them the need to get professional assistance to eliminate the mold and mildew in the room. Grace and Ed cautioned that failure to eliminate the mold and mildew problems immediately could result in serious respiratory health concerns for Andy and the students using the library.

Questions

1. Does the school district have a disaster plan or insurance, and are Andy and the principal familiar with them?
2. Are the custodians familiar with the plan? Should they be? Why?
3. How will Andy find professionals who can help with the mold and mildew problems?
4. Why did Grace and Ed suggest that salvage was not an option? What risk is there in waiting another few days to begin the removal of materials and the elimination of mold and mildew?
5. If the public school district is self-insured, how should Andy proceed?
6. How much of this could have been eliminated or controlled if Andy had been on the scene earlier?
7. How responsible for prevention and cleaning/repairing is a ten-month school staffer like Andy for incidents like this that occur in the summer?

4.2. Purposeful Furniture Purchases or Just a Shopping Spree?

Every elementary school in the district has just received $6,000 for physical plant renovation and furniture purchases. This money is to be used at the discretion of the library media specialist. He or she is encouraged to work with the principal and a team of teachers to decide upon what will be purchased, create a time line, identify vendors/suppliers, and generate the purchase requisitions.

The district received this money from the library foundation. As an urban area with a declining tax base and a growing immigrant population, it barely meets the state standards for purchase of materials. Forget things like furniture, carpeting, and new shelving. The library foundation was quick to recognize the impact on library services that brighter facilities, newer furniture, and the like would have. The library foundation is philosophically focused on decision making at the schools and prefers more bottom-up management as opposed to a top-down model. All purchasing paperwork is submitted to the district's grant coordinator, who will check specifications, solicit bids, set delivery dates, and so on. This administrator will not get involved, however, in the decisions about what to purchase; that is strictly up to the personnel at the school level.

Phou Xiong, who has been the library media specialist at the Matthew Street Elementary School for five years, is thrilled. She has a plan for this money and begins to put it all together. Because she has been at Matthew Street for so long, Phou has a definite idea of the way the room flows, how her traffic patterns occur, and how all of this meshes with her teaching style. She loves the dark oak shelves and the matching circulation desk. She decides to use about $500 to purchase cleaning materials, stain, and varnish. With these supplies in hand, she approaches a friend of hers at the high school. She offers pizza, soda, and an afternoon at the movies to her friend, who teaches industrial arts. In exchange he and some of his students will clean up the wood. The deal is made, leaving Phou with $5,500 of the original funds.

Next, Phou purchases tables and chairs for the instructional portion of the library media center. Phou decides on chairs that are solid oak but lighter in finish than the shelves. The chairs have a shelf underneath for holding binders and other student materials. The tables she selects have pedestal legs and light oak formica tops and are very solid. The cost includes delivery and assembly. Phou also buys several units that are a combination of bins and shelving. These low units have wheels that can be removed and will be used to place books being held on reserve, books for display, and titles that will be more easily accessible for the younger students. Her money is now spent.

During the next few months, the purchases are made and the furniture arrives. Phou, the faculty, and principal are euphoric with the new look. The children love the furniture and make numerous comments. Phou is pleased with her purchases and with the refurbishment of the shelves and the circulation desk. The initial impact to the library media center is a positive one. It exudes order, care, and a sense of purpose.

Members of the library foundation make a site visit to Matthew Street and seem to echo Phou's sentiments. They are pleased with the purchases and their positive impact upon library users. In talking with the faculty, students, and principal it is clear that the foundation's goals of having a team from the school involved have paid off. There is much more ownership of the library media center than before. Everyone seems to have a stake in the appearance and that is now spreading to the library media center's programs as well.

During the coming year, Phou has the opportunity to visit other sites where new furniture was acquired. At one school the funds were used for tables and stools. The tables look like card tables and the stools are very lightweight. The stools can easily tip over and are not at all appropriate for adults. Phou wonders why the school team selected such items. The library media specialist loves them and got such a great price that she was also able to buy new mini-blinds for all of the windows as well as some modular shelving units for paperbacks. At another site Phou is quite taken aback. The furniture is old; in fact, it is very old and in deplorable condition. Standing in the center of the room, however, is a brand-new, very large, circulation desk. The library media specialist proudly explains that now the children feel they have a "real library." She tells Phou that she plans on exploring other funds for tables and chairs but really wanted a professional circulation area. At the third site Phou visits she sees old tables and chairs but a new glass-enclosed bulletin board case in the corridor and wall-to-wall carpeting on the floor. The library media specialist tells Phou that she always hated the hardwood floor and the carpeting makes the center much quieter—just like a real library.

Phou wonders what the library foundation thought of all of the other sites. She wonders what impact these types of bottom-up decisions will have on the future funding of projects through the library foundation.

Questions

1. Whose role is it to decide if furniture is appropriate or not for the library media center?
2. Is the library foundation right to encourage bottom-up decision making as opposed to top-down?
3. Should the foundation have provided technical assistance to ensure furniture decisions were made with greater consideration of what is and is not appropriate?
4. Should the district have made some effort to provide technical assistance?

5. Was any thought given to the longevity and maintenance of the furniture purchased? Is this important?
6. What is the role of the library media supervisor in this type of purchasing?

4.3. The Sky Is Falling: Asbestos Pervades

For several years, a white powdery substance has been falling from the ceiling in the corridors at St. Henry's Elementary School. The ceilings are high enough so that the children can't touch them even if they jump. The powder just falls down and by the end of some days there is enough fine powder on the floors to make them slightly slippery. Johnson Tubb, the head custodian, feels that more and more powder is coming down, and he finally tells Sister Katharine, the principal. Sister decides to call in a contractor to look at putting up ceiling tiles in the halls during the coming summer.

Tucker Wells, the contractor, is a member of St. Henry's Parish and his two boys attend the school. Tucker has been to the school many times but never noticed the powdery substance. Tucker stops by one day and takes a look. He talks with Johnson Tubb and with Sister Katharine. He looks at the building plans and then tells Sister the problem.

St. Henry's was built in 1955. The ceiling is made of asbestos mixed with plaster. This added an element of soundproofing to the corridors. Now, with the passage of forty-plus years, a new roof last year, an unusually cold winter followed by a sweltering summer, the situation is worse than ever before. Tucker tells Sister Katharine that the ceilings need to be replaced or covered immediately and that he cannot do the work. He also informs her that the powdery substance is asbestos and that an abatement company, specially licensed, must be hired immediately. Sister notifies the pastor and immediate action is taken.

The next two weeks are frantic ones for the faculty at St. Henry's. The abatement project will commence but school will continue. The company that has been hired specializes in school asbestos removal and will sequence their work on selected sections of the building. They will work from 4 P.M. until 4 A.M., Monday through Friday, and twenty-four hours on Saturday. Halls and ceilings will be curtained off with plastic. Decontamination areas will be clearly identified. Asbestos removal signs will be posted and areas under work will be closed off. The health department is involved, along with the contractor.

Suki Matsuso is the library media specialist at St. Henry's. She's worked there for several years and loves her job. The library media center is on the top floor and is quite large—about the size of two and one-half classrooms. The room is airy, the furniture new, and the ceiling is falling. Suki's room was designed originally to double as the music room and hence the same ceiling material used in the corridors was used in the library media center. Suki is nonplussed by the amount of work facing her and the disruption to her facility. She knows that the company doing the work will work with her; she's already talked to the foreman and the manager.

The abatement project begins in the first-floor corridor. Signs to enter and leave the building are posted and traffic patterns changed. All staff must leave by 4 P.M. When they arrive each morning the floors have been washed and monitors are placed strategically around the building. Readings are taken on a twice-daily basis by the health department. Everything flows smoothly.

At the end of the first month, the work moves into the library media center. Suki has put away everything that was on the top of shelves, file cabinets, desks, and any flat surfaces. She has removed posters and wall hangings. The furniture and any freestanding items are removed from the room by Johnson Tubb and the shelves sealed in plastic. The library media center will be closed for one week while the asbestos ceiling is contained and a new drop ceiling installed. During the week Suki conducts story telling in the lower-grade classrooms and does some cooperative teaching with the intermediate-grade teachers. On Friday, she talks with the foreman, who tells her she can be back in her room on Monday.

Monday morning Suki arrives at St. Henry's at 7:30 A.M. She has no illusions about what she will find. When she gets to the room, however, she is horrified. The furniture is dumped in the middle of the room and several chairs are damaged. The plastic has been removed from the shelves but the floors have not been washed. Many books are on the floor; some seem to be covered in white powder. One of the locked file cabinets containing the video collection has been forced open and many items are missing. Suki immediately contacts Sister Katharine and Johnson Tubb. Together the three of them meet with the foreman and the manager of the abatement company. As time goes on, the library media center is restored to its former condition. Suki works hard to achieve that and often comes in on Saturdays. The abatement continues in other parts of the building. That winter, with the forced-air heat turned on and the windows closed, Suki and other teachers contract a variety of upper respiratory ailments.

Questions

1. Was the faculty briefed about the potential hazards to health and materials? Who should have been responsible for this?
2. Was covering the bookshelves with plastic sufficient protection? What other methods could have been used?
3. How did some of the books land on the floor and get covered with powder?
4. Who supervised the cleanup and moving of the furniture back into the library media center? Was that a thorough plan?
5. Who is responsible for the loss of videos and damage to furniture?
6. Was it appropriate to conduct full-scale abatement while the building was still being used as a school?
7. Should the library media center have been closed for the semester?
8. Should the heating system have been upgraded or cleaned so that the fine asbestos particles had no chance to be dispersed and cause illness?

4.4. Czar of the Copier Machine

For years, the teachers at Central Day Academy have been asking for a copier. They find that more and more teaching materials are available on black-lined masters and they are spending large amounts of personal dollars making copies at local stores. There are still stencil machines and ditto machines, but no high-speed copiers are available in the building. Patrice Mansour, the headmistress at Central, sympathizes with the faculty and finally convinces the board to allocate money toward any type of copier that will do high-speed, high-volume copying.

After requesting bids, a decision is made and a Lackner machine is installed in the library media center at Central. The Lackner is a combined electronic stencil maker and high-speed copier. Patrice makes the decision to house it in the center without consulting with the library media specialist. During the summer, the secretaries in the office and the administrative staff learn how to use the Lackner. With the start of school in September, Jennifer Hernandez, the library media specialist, is surprised to find the Lackner in the library media center. She stops by Patrice's office to inquire about its placement but is stopped short by faculty enthusiasm over its acquisition. The placement of the machine seems secondary and of importance only to Jennifer.

During the first week of school Jennifer is busy with her open flexible library schedule. She is meeting with teachers, setting up the computers, placing new books on the shelf, and booking classes. During her meetings with the teachers she does find it handy to have the Lackner in the center. After the first few days she has trained most of the faculty in the rudiments of operating the machine and adjusts to having it in the library media center. She is a bit put out, however, that Patrice never consulted her nor even told her about its pending location.

The Lackner is all that its publicity says it is—quiet, reliable, and a workhorse. Because it is in the library media center, Jennifer has the opportunity to see what the teachers are copying and to suggest print and nonprint sources to supplement their lessons. Circulation is up and there are more opportunities to interact with the faculty. Because she sees firsthand what the faculty is copying, Jennifer is more involved in the instructional process than ever before.

By the third week of the semester, Jennifer's schedule is filled with cooperative lessons, book talks, and circulating materials. She is often interrupted, however, during her lessons to diagnose some difficulty with the Lackner. She quickly solves each problem but resents the intrusion. Often, teachers will come over to the instructional area of the library media center just to ask her advice about making double-sided copies or reducing something to fit on a page. She answers but her voice sends a different message. Jennifer also has to worry about stocking supplies (paper and ink) for the Lackner. When the machine is running low on supplies, it beeps continuously until the problem is corrected. This chronic beeping is another intrusion into Jennifer's day.

Each morning Jennifer comes into the library media center about an hour early. She brings up the computer network, checks in magazines, has her coffee, and generally prepares herself mentally for the day's activities. She reviews her schedule and may even read some book reviews.

Now, with the Lackner in the center, she is greeted by chattering faculty who want to dither on about nothing while their copies are shooting out of the machine. Jennifer finds this disruption to her routine annoying. The same type of interference is happening at the end of the day as well. Jennifer keeps the library media center open about an hour each day after school. Generally, students come in to do homework, wait for a ride, or engage in some quiet research. Jennifer uses this time to pick up the center after the day's events and to prepare for the next day. Now, that routine is disrupted for many of the same reasons.

Jennifer finds herself staying later each day and getting less done. She enjoys the social atmosphere of having the faculty in the library media center and the closer working relationship she has with them. After Christmas, however, she decides the Lackner has to go. She will talk with Patrice about putting it in the workroom across the hall. There is no electricity there but that's a problem that is easy to correct.

Questions

1. If circulation is up and more teachers are using the library media center, what's the problem?
2. Should Jennifer set up a schedule for using the copier and eliminate the interruptions to her classes and preparation/cleanup time?
3. What problem is created by the faculty socializing in the library media center?
4. Who should have been consulted about placing the copier in the library media center?
5. If the copier is moved across the hall, will that solve the problems that Jennifer has or just move them further away? What will prevent faculty from continuing to disrupt her class?
6. Should Jennifer offer to copy the faculty's materials herself on a daily basis and make them available within a certain time frame? Should someone else, such as a student/volunteer be assigned this task to eliminate Jennifer's interruptions?

5

District, Regional, and State Leadership

5.1. Inventory—The Dreaded "I" Word

For the last three years, library media specialists in the Princely Town School District have not conducted the annual inventory of their collections. This inventory is mandated by some out-of-date regulations from the State Department of Education. This regulation has been used in the past to give the library media specialists five days without scheduled classes at the end of the school year.

Three years ago the practice was stopped when a classroom teacher at the Robertson Elementary School filed a grievance. Her contention was that the children were being deprived of library services at the end of the school year and that this was unfair not only to the children but to the classroom teachers as well. During the five inventory days the library classes were covered by a substitute teacher and were held in the homerooms. The library media specialist was working on inventory in the library media center, which was closed to borrowers. The school committee sided with the teacher and the library media specialists were not given the five days at the end of the school year to conduct the inventory. On the advice of one of the more vocal school library media specialists, no specialist from Princely conducted inventory and the State Education Department was notified that the schools were out of compliance.

Eventually, the superintendent of Princely tired of hearing from the district supervisor about the inventory situation. He was inundated with petty grievances from the library media specialists about their lack of time for weeding, book and equipment repairs, collection mapping, and other inventory-related activities. An adversarial relationship between the district supervisor and the school library media specialists often turned nasty at their monthly meetings. Although strictly speaking the library media specialists were not "working to rule," their attitude toward any type of activity not specified in the contract spoke volumes about their unhappiness. At a social gathering the superintendent spoke with Gracia Vega, the most vocal of the school library media specialists, about settling the issues related to inventory and end-of-the-year activities. He asked Gracia to poll her colleagues and come up with some strategies and time lines that would make everyone happy.

Gracia sent a letter to the forty school library media specialists affected by the inventory impasse. This included all elementary and middle school specialists but not those in the high schools. With their flexible schedules and full-time clerical assistants, inventory was not an issue for the high school's media specialists. In her letter, Gracia asked the specialists to meet with her after school one day to discuss solutions, develop a time line for implementation, and get a survey of her colleagues about how to proceed.

On the date suggested, nearly all of the affected library media specialists gathered at Gracia's school. After much vocalizing of concerns about past inequities and difficulties, Gracia finally focused the group on the inventory situation. She divided the group into elementary and middle schools and then divided each of those groups into those with on-line catalogs and those without. She asked each of these four groups to come up with a plan to implement the state-mandated process. She informed the group that the superintendent was unable to overrule the settlement won by the teacher from Robertson. In other words, five days at the end of the school year with a substitute covering scheduled classes in the homerooms was not an option.

At the end of the meeting, the group decided that one person from each of the four smaller groups would constitute a writing committee. These four library media specialists plus Gracia would draft a proposal and bring it back within thirty days to the larger group. This proposal would include specific language about the procedures of the inventory, training for those with and without on-line automation, and a time line for implementation. The larger group would then vote and the document would be submitted to the superintendent. As the group adjourned, there was a sense of satisfaction that things were finally moving forward.

Questions

1. What is the purpose of an annual inventory?
2. Is closing the library media center during the last five days of school the most effective way to conduct an inventory?
3. What should the district supervisor do to settle this issue?
4. Was it the most appropriate way for the superintendent to settle this issue?
5. What kinds of plans could the five library media specialists develop? What proven options are available?
6. Where is the bargaining union in all of this, and what is its role?

5.2. The Library Checking Account: Who Uses It, Why, and for What?

Each year Vanthy Thach, the library media specialist at Capstone Elementary School, raises a significant amount of money for her library media center. She does this by book fairs, Parent Teacher Organization (PTO) donations, raffles, direct mailings, and even some grants. At any given moment the funds available to Vanthy number about $1,500. Vanthy is scrupulous with her record keeping for this account. She has a loose-leaf notebook with three columns: income, expenses, and source of funds or disbursements. In addition, she keeps everything up to date, recording any activity at the moment it occurs. Vanthy keeps the money in cash in her coat closet, and no one, not even the principal or the district supervisor, is aware of its existence. It isn't as though Vanthy is trying to hide the money; they all know she has money and that she raises it in a variety of ways. It is just that people don't ever ask her how she handles it.

Last September Vanthy met a woman on the airplane coming back from a conference who told her that her bank offered free checking accounts to nonprofit agencies. She suggested that Vanthy open an account with her "petty cash," as she called it. She told Vanthy that having a checking account made purchases easier to track and removed any sense of impropriety about the money. She suggested to Vanthy that keeping everything in cash not only made it easier to steal but might raise questions in people's eyes about fund sources, expenses, and so on. After thinking it over, Vanthy opened an account at the Princely Savings Bank. She deposited $1,800 in cash and ordered two hundred checks imprinted with "The Library, Capstone Elementary School." Vanthy listed herself as the signatory on the account and used the school's tax-exemption number for identification purposes.

About ten days later the checks arrived in the mail. Vanthy felt that she had moved into the twentieth century. She would now be able to order things and have them invoiced and shipped. She would then pay by check instead of putting the money into her personal account and writing a personal check to pay for what she wanted to buy or, worse, getting a money order at the post office. With the imprinted checks, Vanthy was able to open an account at each of the two major bookstores in Princely. Now she could order items over the phone, pick them up on her way home from work, and pay by check when invoiced.

Last week Vanthy received a small grant from the local chamber of commerce. They funded her request to purchase some lounge furniture for part of the reading room. She plans to purchase a love seat, a rocker, a coffee table, and some cushions. The grant is for $2,500 with anything left over after buying the furniture to be used for books. Vanthy promptly deposits the funds into her checking account and scans the local paper for furniture sales.

At the monthly meeting of the school library media specialists it is customary for each person to have a moment to highlight something that is occurring in their library media center. Vanthy uses this as an opportunity to tell her colleagues about her new checking account. She brings forms for each of them to complete and provides them with a copy of the district's tax-exemption certificate. Vanthy tells her colleagues just how simple it is to make purchases, keep track of small grants, and even generate reports about income and expenditures. She explains that she now has no need to bother the front office for a check from the principal or to get a money order at the post office when making a purchase. The other school library media specialists listen attentively and eagerly take the forms. Jack Gallant, the library media supervisor, sits and listens to Vanthy's presentation with his mouth open. He cannot believe what he's just heard. When the group takes a few minutes for a coffee break, he tells Vanthy that he wants to speak with her privately.

Questions

1. Should the library media specialist have access to her own petty cash?
2. Should this account have been opened using the district's tax-exempt certificate but with only Vanthy's name and not someone higher up in the organization as a co-signer?
3. Most school library media centers generate funds through the PTO, book fairs, fines, lost books, and so on. How should these funds be handled?
4. With Vanthy as the only signatory on the account, can issues of fiscal mismanagement arise?
5. How can checks and balances on this account be created and maintained with minimum paperwork?
6. What is the role of the district supervisor in this issue?
7. Should the policy manual for the school district address the issues that arise in this case?

5.3. "I Just Needed These Titles for a Unit I'm Doing; No One Else Was Using Them"

Jerry Avila is currently working as the school library media specialist at the Northwood Elementary School. Northwood is in a suburban district just outside of the city of Portway. Portway is a large city with about forty elementary schools. Jerry worked at one of these schools, Winston Elementary, for about three years. Jerry liked Winston but really wanted to leave Portway and work in one of the suburban towns near where he lived. When the Northwood position opened up, he was ecstatic. This was his dream job—an elementary school with a flexible schedule and a district committed to resource-based instruction. Jerry accepted the job and got a $5,000 raise in the process.

Jerry keeps in touch with his colleagues at Portway but doesn't miss the fixed schedule of classes nor the disruptive kids. Slowly, he is building his collection at Northwood and goes out of his way to get materials for units and themes in his building. The teachers at his new school love him and his colleagues in Portway miss his wit and knowledge of children's literature.

Last night about 8:30, Jerry's replacement, Gretchen Bartlett, called a friend of hers about something that Jerry has been doing. This friend was Jerry's supervisor when he did his practicum in the master of library science (MLS) program and has kept in touch with Jerry, even writing him a recommendation for the new job at Northwood. This friend, Jack Weiss, was absolutely stunned by the news he received. It seems that Jerry has been going into Winston Elementary after hours. He has been let in on several occasions by the school custodian, once by a teacher who was staying late herself, and twice by the school nurse, who was leaving as Jerry was coming in. Gretchen goes on to tell Jack that the principal at Winston is very upset about this and has complained both to Human Resources and to the district supervisor about Jerry's "unlawful entry." Gretchen tells Jack that the district is considering having Jerry arrested for trespassing the next time.

Jack is absolutely dumbfounded. He tells Gretchen that he will call Jerry and talk with him. He cannot imagine what Jerry has been doing at Winston after hours. After all, he left Winston nearly a year ago. Perhaps, he thinks, Jerry left personal files there and now realizes it. Not wanting to bother Gretchen, whom he doesn't know, he just goes in after school. This is troubling to Jack, however. He thinks Jerry should let the principal and Gretchen know about his presence as a courtesy. Jack assures Gretchen that he will sort this out and keep her name out of it.

Jack calls Jerry immediately. They chat for a few minutes about generalities and then Jack tells Jerry what he's heard. He further tells Jerry that he might be arrested the next time he goes in to Winston. Jerry says he doesn't know why anyone is making such a big deal about it. Jerry tells Jack how he did such a great job building the collection at Winston. He claims that Gretchen isn't using some of the units that Jerry had bought materials for. Since they were just sitting there and Jerry could use them at his new school, he just went in to borrow them. Jack asks Jerry if he signed them out and Jerry says no. Jack is confused and appalled. Jerry has just admitted stealing from Winston. Jerry says he has "borrowed" about twelve picture books and a few books on states. Jerry says he will return them right away and Jack cautions him to stay away from the building. Jack says he can return them to Winston in the school mail delivery. That way, no one will know where they have come from and who had them. Jerry agrees and delivers the materials in new, unmarked, manila envelopes to Jack's home the next night. The next morning, Jack begins to mail the books back to Winston.

Questions

1. Was Jack right to get involved with this or should he have left this issue for the district supervisor?
2. Does one underhanded act (removing the books surreptitiously) beget another (returning them anonymously)?
3. Was the principal correct in notifying Human Resources and the district supervisor, or should he have called Jerry directly, as Jack did?
4. Are there ethical considerations here in addition to the theft and trespassing ones?

5.4. The Volunteer with the Pipeline

Irene Tilyson is the parent of a troublesome student at Nativity Elementary School. Irene's daughter, Ursula, is loud, uncooperative, and generally disruptive in class. Ursula is particularly disruptive in the library media center, where she and Mr. Edey, the library media supervisor, never see eye to eye. Ursula is often sent from the library to the principal's office and assigned detention because of her behavior. Numerous calls to her mother have not changed the situation. When the year ends, Mr. Edey is relieved that he won't have Ursula in class again.

With the start of the new school year, Mr. Edey notifies the principal that he would like a volunteer in the library. The volunteer would process new books, file shelflist inventory cards, and do some light typing and other clerical tasks. Mr. Edey has always had at least one parent each semester to help in the library. Generally, the parents are ones whose children really enjoy coming to the library either during the open times or the class periods. This year, Mr. Edey is quite surprised when Mrs. Tilyson signs up to be the parent volunteer in the library.

Mr. Edey goes immediately to the principal to see what precipitated

Mrs. Tilyson's interest in serving as a volunteer in the library media center. The principal is not sure and tells Mr. Edey that this is the first time that Mrs. Tilyson has volunteered for anything. The principal then checks the form that Mrs. Tilyson completed and notes that she did specify that she was only available to work in the library media center. With some trepidation, Mr. Edey calls Mrs. Tilyson to confirm that she will be working in the library media center and to set up a mutually acceptable schedule.

Mrs. Tilyson arrives promptly on the days agreed to. She works diligently on the tasks assigned and is most agreeable. She and Mr. Edey develop a camaraderie. Mrs. Tilyson is often working when Mr. Edey has classes in the library media center. At first Mr. Edey is quite self-conscious about her presence but gradually he grows accustomed to it. She never comments about his classes, their decorum, or his management of them. After a while he grows comfortable with her presence in the room while he is teaching. Once in a while he will roll his eyes or shake his head in her direction when something is out of sync in his class. She generally responds in a similar manner.

Each day during the second teaching period, there is a group of teachers who gather in the library media center to read the paper and drink coffee. This is their unassigned period and the library media center has no scheduled class for that teaching period. The four teachers are fifth- and sixth-grade teachers with a number of years of experience at Nativity Elementary. They often discuss problems in their classes and assist one another with lessons. They do plan cooperatively during this time, but this is not considered their official planning time. Lately, the conversation among the four teachers has focused on issues that affect the faculty at Nativity. These center on the lack of adequate supplies for the math department, especially in the area of manipulative objects that students can use for calculations. This topic then leads to a discussion of general funding for texts, supplemental materials, computers, and so on. To the casual observer this seems like so much unhappiness, but in reality these teachers often come up with creative solutions to the problems that are raised. Mr. Edey is generally working with Mrs. Tilyson during this time period, but he will often interject some thoughts into their conversation.

Last week the conversation focused on several girls in the sixth grade who are dressing inappropriately. Comments were made to the girls' parents, but nothing has changed. The four teachers discuss what to do and how perhaps each will make an appointment to talk individually with the parents. On Monday, Sook, the principal, comes into the library to talk with Mr. Edey. She indicates that the library media center seems to be the gossip center for the school. Teachers hang out there, and Mr. Edey has set a tone in the library media center that is conducive to idle chatter and disrespect for the school and its mission. The principal indicates that she has notified the diocesan library media supervisor that a review of Mr. Edey's schedule is warranted.

Further, she expects that a reprimand for allowing teachers to hang out in the library media center will be placed into his personnel file. Mr. Edey is shocked at what the principal is saying. He feels he has done nothing wrong and wonders who has been talking about what occurs in the library media center. He immediately suspects Mrs. Tilyson.

Questions

1. Was Mr. Edey right to allow the teachers to hang out in the library media center during their free periods?
2. Assuming Mrs. Tilyson has been talking about what she's heard in the library media center, should the principal have spoken with Mr. Edey before going to the diocesan library media supervisor?
3. What role, if any, should Mr. Edey have played in allowing teacher conversations to occur in the presence of Mrs. Tilyson?
4. Is it Mr. Edey's responsiblity to have told Mrs. Tilyson that whatever she hears within the context of her volunteer time is considered confidential?
5. Assuming that Mrs. Tilyson spoke with the principal or someone else in authority, was the principal right in giving credence to her comments or should she have proceeded in another fashion?
6. Do the teachers involved have any method of recourse because their professional privacy has been violated?

II

MIDDLE OR JUNIOR HIGH SCHOOL LIBRARY MEDIA CENTERS

6

Leadership, Planning, and Management

6.1. Let's Get Organized—Time Management on the Job

Mickey Bennefeld is overwhelmed. As the only library media specialist at Mercy Junior High School in Toldank, he must balance reference, book selection, cataloging, systems analysis, and the like each day. The girls at Mercy just adore Mickey—he is always there to help when they've put off their term papers. They respect him and find in him a good friend. Many keep in touch as they go on to high school and college, and he receives tons of e-mail from grateful graduates. He also receives numerous requests for information for high school and college assignments from these same grateful grads. Mickey is happy in his career. He has been at Mercy for fifteen years and the time has flown by. The school is noted throughout the region for its strong academic program as well as for its winning basketball team. Mickey feels that he is a member of a winning faculty team.

This year, the school was reviewed for accreditation. The self-study took a year and Mickey chaired the Building Facilities Committee. He worked closely with his committee and their report was well received. Just prior to the visit by the Regional Review Committee, Mickey came in on a Saturday to clean up the library media center. One of the plant maintenance men was also working that Saturday—waxing the front hall and cleaning the auditorium. Mickey sorted through the piles of mail that came in during the last month when he was busy with the Facilities Committee. He checked in magazines and filed them. He put some things in the vertical file and checked in about one hundred titles that had been sitting on a book cart. He shelved the books and straightened up the public portion of the library. Mickey then looked in his office/processing room and decided to pack everything up in boxes and put them in his car trunk. This way, he rationalized, the initial impression is that the room is neat and the workflow orderly. Mickey plans to deal with the problems in the boxes in his trunk after the accreditation visit.

Mickey got some paper boxes from the back closet and began to pack. After about an hour and a half, order was restored and six full boxes were ready to move out. In addition, two wastebaskets were also filled. Mickey decided to go to the deli to get a sandwich. On his way out he asked Jack from plant maintenance to empty the wastebaskets in the library and his office and also offered to bring Jack a sandwich.

Mickey is gone for about an hour—he has run into some of Mercy's recent graduates at the deli and stayed for coffee with them. Upon his return, he and Jack have their sandwiches and talk about Friday night's game. Mickey then tells Jack he's going to put some stuff in his car. Upon entering the library media center, Mickey realizes that Jack has emptied the wastebaskets and also tossed out the boxes of work that Mickey was going to store in his trunk.

Fortunately, there is no harm done. The boxes have been stacked by the elevator for transport to the dumpster. Mickey retrieves them and puts them in his trunk. On the way home, Mickey resolves never to let the paperwork back up like this again.

During the summer months, Mickey lives up to his resolution. He comes in for two weeks and reorganizes his workflow, his office, and his procedures. Mickey creates logs for books, equipment, and patrons; he creates a blank form for classes to use when they want to schedule time in the library; he has a conference planning log, a processing log, and a folder for memos to and from the faculty and to and from the principal. He develops a project file, a tickler file, an action file, a to-do file, and a subscription file. Mickey has everything labeled and color coded. His office looks like it could be used in a catalog for library or office supplies.

When school starts, the faculty meeting takes place in the library. Teachers and staff alike stop and comment on Mickey's new look—he has a plant on his desk and a small oriental carpet in his office. His computer has a cover and he has bought covers for all of the machines on his network. Everything is spotless. Mickey basks in the glow of recognition. His hard work has not been in vain.

When the students return the next day they descend on the library media center to renew acquaintances with Mickey. As the days go by, the center moves into full swing—reference searches, team teaching, bibliographic instruction, circulation of materials, requests for copies, help with homework, and the like. At the end of each day, Mickey is frazzled. He is trying to keep his various systems going but is staying later and later to do so. His files are a mess and he is losing things—a memo from the principal, a request from the Parent Teacher Association (PTO). He worked so hard and things looked so good. Now what is he to do?

Questions

1. Does Mickey have the right components to manage his library media center efficiently? What is missing, if anything?
2. Should he stop some of the activities he does now (such as e-mail correspondence with the graduates) so that he has more time to manage the present demands on the center?
3. Is the issue time management, or is the load impossible for only one library media specialist in a center that is so active? Is there a position here for student volunteers? Would a full-time clerk help?
4. Would closing down during the lunch period help to catch up? What if he closed down during his free period? What other options would help Mickey with his management problem?
5. Is much of what Mickey is doing with his new system just moving paperwork around, or is he really managing more effectively?
6. Will a wait-and-see attitude help?

6.2. Professional Responsibility or Just Keeping Up?

Sally Malcolm has been a library media specialist for two years in the rural community of Benning. She was a technician for about five years at a public library before beginning her family. While her children were young she decided to get her master of library science degree (MLS) and train for work as a school library media specialist. Sally works full time at the Jason Junior High in Benning and has been there for one semester. Sally transferred from Samuels Junior High because of health reasons; she has terrible asthma and the old Samuels building with its sixty-five years of dust and mold was just too much for her.

Sally is a hard worker but never sure of herself. She has difficulty taking charge of a project. She is more content to live from day to day and often fails to see the results that her action or lack of action creates. Rather than take the initiative, she will work for consensus on an issue. She is very comfortable with the highly structured school administration and feels no need to be a trailblazer in her profession.

Sally's colleagues like her, and fellow teachers at Samuels were sad when she left. Sally inherits a poor collection at Jason Junior High, but it offers an on-line catalog and about a three-quarters flexible schedule. She is friendly to the children and fairly knowledgeable about computer search strategies. However, there is something wrong with the on-line catalog and she's not sure how to fix it. She can still check books out, but the on-line computer search stations show that a lot of stuff is missing. In fact, about every book that Sally looks for shows as missing on the search screen but is actually on the shelf. Sally notices that when the book is checked out, an error message appears on the circulation screen. When the book is checked back in, however, everything is just fine again. Sally plans to ask her library supervisor for assistance when she gets things more organized. Although she pays for technical support for her on-line catalog, she doesn't want to bother the vendor with her problems. She hopes to be able to work around them for a while and hopes that eventually they'll go away.

In addition to what Sally calls a "little glitch" in the on-line catalog, there are about 1,000 pre-printed bar codes stuffed in a drawer. There are also about the same number of books without bar codes on shelves around the circulation desk. She has no idea whether they will match up or not. There was no inventory done prior to automating, and a glance at the sheets of bar codes makes her wonder if any of these books have been on the shelves at Jason within the last twenty years. Sally feels that in time she will get to these "little difficulties." Meanwhile, Sally has a visiting author program to organize, children to teach, and faculty to work with so that her flexible schedule is justified.

The principal at Jason, a so-so library advocate, is concerned about the initial appearance of the room and talks to Sally about sprucing things up. Sally takes his words to heart and has the children make paper leaves and snow flakes for decorations. She thinks that ordering book trucks to store the "little difficulties" on and displaying some bright posters will help. The principal authorizes money for one large book truck and the PTO gives her a gift certificate at the local frame shop.

When the book truck arrives, Sally puts the books with no bar codes either on it or in cartons under her desk. She labels the books and cartons "no bar codes." She now has some blank shelves on which to display new titles. She also brings in some plastic chairs to lend a casual atmosphere to one end of the room and then she continues business as usual. She concentrates heavily on teaching skills to the classes and plans to focus on integrated, thematic units. At the end of the first quarter, the circulation figures are down and the faculty is not using the library. Both groups of patrons—students and staff—are frustrated by how the on-line catalog and the shelves do not correlate. Senior teachers say that the computer is at fault, while others claim that Sally must have thrown out many volumes and not cleared up the records. Sally suffers silently and never tells them about the bar codes without books or the books without bar codes. Sally never speaks to her supervisor about the computer problem. The principal is out on leave following an auto accident, so speaking to him is not an option. Six months after arriving at Jason Junior High, Sally's family is transferred away from Benning. Sally leaves the library pretty much as she found it but with copious notes about the problems and glitches.

Questions

1. What responsibility has Sally accepted for the mess she's inherited? Whom should she have alerted to these issues?
2. Should she develop a plan with a time line to match up the books and bar codes and fix whatever is wrong with the on-line catalog?
3. Do school library media specialists have a professional responsibility to not only manage classes and schedules but handle computer problems, inherited backlogs of processing, cataloging, and so on?
4. Which is more important—handling the backlogs or dealing with the present patron and his/her information needs?
5. Is there a correlation between the appearance of the room and the use of the collection?
6. Who should the faculty tell about Sally's errors or the problem with the computer?

6.3. You Can't Go Home Again: Ethics of Peer Intervention

After employing substitute library media specialists for two years, the Middleburgh Middle School is finally getting a permanent person. The new library media specialist, Cleotilde Tomas-Castro has the most seniority, wants the position, and transfers to Middleburgh at the start of the semester. She's been in about eleven schools in the last nine years, but as she tells everyone, she was just waiting for the right placement. Middleburgh is just what she's been looking for, and she hopes to stay there forever. There is a lot to like about Middleburgh—a balanced collection of nine thousand volumes, subscriptions to about fifty periodicals, an on-line catalog, three stand-alone CD workstations, access to the Web, and a pleasant work space. The school population is eight hundred, and all grades are teamed for academic instruction. There is an advisor/advisee program in place, an active PTO, and partnerships with the local university. There is also a lot not to like about Middleburgh—a fixed schedule, lunch and bus duty, and no correlation between the library skills classes and the academic classroom. The teachers at Middleburgh love their library but don't think of it as anything other than as supplement to their texts. There is heavy circulation by the faculty but no joint presentation of lessons. Generally the day before a teacher wants to present a lesson, he or she sends up a note and asks to borrow an assortment of resources on a particular topic. The concepts of resource-based instruction, flexible scheduling, and cooperative lessons are not part of this library, and Cleotilde faces a lot of challenges if she decides to break the trends. Cleotilde comes in the first day of school and surveys the library. She moves a lot of things around but doesn't seem bothered by the boxes of unpacked and unprocessed books that are about. She wants to know where the lunchroom is, what days she has bus duty,and when the other elective/special subject teachers have bus and lunch duty. She leaves promptly at 3:00.

As the month progresses, Cleotilde arrives and leaves exactly on time. Her classes are skill oriented, and she has difficulty managing the children. By her own admission her lessons run short—she finishes presenting the skills before the class period is over. She's not sure what to do with the students during the last few minutes of class and tries to insist that they sit silently, waiting for the bell. She writes many discipline referrals and speaks daily to the assistant principal about problem students. In the lunchroom she complains about teaching so many classes.

The teachers continue to patronize the library individually but don't bring their classes in or schedule cooperative lessons. They continue to borrow materials and set up small classroom libraries in their homerooms that are subject specific to the theme or lesson of the time. Cleotilde seems undisturbed by this.

At the end of the semester, the circulation is about the same as in the past, and the library opens and closes on time. There are no new bulletin boards or bibliographies, and the boxes of unprocessed books remain unpacked. The mail seems to pile up and the general appearance of the room is not inviting. Cleotilde seems unsure of how to deal with the many facets of the job and flits from one task to another, never completing anything. The principal, Albertina Johnson, asks Cleotilde about the new materials, but Cleotilde tells her there just isn't enough time in the day for all of the work.

Marian Phong was the former library media specialist. She was at Middleburgh for five years until leaving to care for her mother. Marian has been gone from the district for three years. Upon her return she finds that she has a position in Centerville but not at Middleburgh. Marian worked wonders with the fixed schedule at Middleburgh, opening before school for the teachers and students and making the library an important part of the instructional process. Because of her commitment to the concept of flexible scheduling, progress was being made in that direction. The teachers were beginning to work cooperatively with her and Marian thought that perhaps in a year or so the whole schedule might turn around. Marian and Albertina became friends during Marian's five-year tenure.

Albertina has supper one evening with Marian and mentions Cleotilde and the library. Marian listens and what she hears confirms what other faculty have told her. Marian is angry that the circumstances of the teacher contract prevented her from returning to "her" school. She is horrified to have confirmation that the "babysitter" librarian is holding down the job at Middleburgh. Furthermore, the books that have come in during the last few years are just sitting there, the before and after school programs are gone, no bibliographies are being generated, and the bulletin boards are still the ones Marian created before she left. Marian offers to help Albertina by coming out to Middleburgh to look things over. She tells Albertina that she will come in one Saturday when no one is around. Albertina and she agree on a date, and they meet in the parking lot that morning.

Marian is horrified by what she sees at Middleburgh. The place is filthy and the shelves are in complete disarray. She is absolutely shocked to look at the library and see what has happened. Some of the posters are falling off the wall, and there are unshelved books everywhere. Some piles of books behind the circulation desk are missing bar codes. The printer is being used as a desk and the computer system's main central processing unit is on its side on the floor. There are dirty coffee cups everywhere, and the mail is piled up on a chair. Marian shares her shock and dismay with Albertina and promises to draw up a plan to get Middleburgh back in shape. Albertina says she has some work to do in her office and suggests that Marian make herself at home and begin to draw up a list of what needs to be done.

Questions

1. What recourse will Cleotilde have if she finds out that Marian has been asked to look at the library media center?
2. Should Albertina have asked Marian to look at the library media center and make recommendations?
3. Does Albertina have a problem in the library, or is she just not adjusting to staff change?
4. Does Cleotilde have a right to arrive and leave for home in conjunction with the school schedule, or is she obligated to teach her classes and stay after to get the rest of the work done?
5. Should Albertina have approached Cleotilde with her concerns?
6. Should Albertina have approached the district supervisor with her concerns?
7. Should the district supervisor have offered help to Cleotilde? Should she have permitted the former library media specialist to come back in a consultant role?
8. What are the ethical considerations here for Albertina? For Marian? For Cleotilde? For the district supervisor?
9. Should Marian have notified Cleotilde that she would be looking at the library media center and suggested that they work together?

6.4. Statistics—Friend or Foe?

Each month Roberto Ocasio prints out circulation statistics from the library's on-line catalog. The report gives facts about the collection—number of titles, number of volumes, circulation by classification, circulation by patron types, and so on. Roberto looks over the data and files the report in his file cabinet. Each quarter he charts the year's data using ClarisWorks and presents the graph to his principal, Dr. Nicola. Roberto also uses the graphs to supplement grant requests and make presentations to the PTO, and he sends a copy to the district supervisor.

Dr. Nicola always comments on the data and usually works in some information about the library media center in his monthly report to the faculty, parents, and central administration. Dr. Nicola has been a principal in several other middle schools and was once an assistant principal in a high school. He is an avid library user and credits Roberto with putting Holly Middle School on the map.

Roberto enjoys his job and not only works hard but works well. The staff and students are always welcome and rarely is a request for information unmet. Roberto is a natural leader but with a style that focuses on consensus. He works with the district supervisor in such a way as to bring about change from within. Roberto is generally thought to be a team player, although he sees himself as an agent of change.

For the last ten years the district supervisor for the library media program has not been a library media specialist by training. Typically these supervisors have been drawn from the ranks of the humanities supervisors. Kathi Sachs has been the supervisor for six years. She is also a natural leader and has not been hampered in her supervision of the library media specialists by her lack of formal training. Kathi is levelheaded and works hard at her job. Through her efforts major changes in staffing, training, and monies have come about. She works in close conjunction with the building principals and considers Roberto to be one of the best library media specialists in the school district. Kathi has just finished her Ph.D. in administration and chooses to leave the district for an out-of-state assistant superintendent position. Replacing her is Frank Borolo. Like Kathi, Frank comes from the ranks of the humanities faculty. Unlike Kathi, Frank is not a hard worker but rather a promiser. The library media specialists call him "Promise Me Frankie." Frank rarely holds meetings or even writes memos. He doesn't get involved in interviewing new staff nor does he take the initiative when it comes to budgets. He is always on the phone or out of town at conferences. Many of the library media specialists under his supervision have never met him.

As the first year in the job winds down for Frank, he hears rumblings from five of the six middle school principals that their libraries, with their flexible schedules and large physical spaces, are underused. The district needs more classroom space and elective teachers are needed to cover the teachers' unassigned periods. The building principals want the library media centers downsized and a return to fixed-schedule programs. Several middle school library media specialists hear of this proposal and get together with Frank. He tells them they have nothing to worry about. He says that he will just continue as in the past and that this is just a way for principals to vent frustrations. They are in dire straits, he explains, and are trying to find ways to handle increasing enrollments.

Roberto is a realist and decides to prepare a way to fight this proposal. He talks with his principal, Dr. Nicola, who says that Holly Middle School's enrollment is fine and that there is no way he would sacrifice the program in the library media center. Roberto feels that his data, coupled with that of the other middle schools, might help to sway the five principals faced with space and enrollment problems. He approaches Frank and reviews his data, suggesting that it could supply a benchmark for the district middle schools. Frank thinks it is a good idea, especially the graphs. He prepares a memo and sends it out to all of the middle school library media specialists. In his memo he shows some of Roberto's data without indicating its source. He asks the five other school library media specialists for similar data. He explains that he will use these facts to fight to save space and schedules.

The data for all six middle schools are sent on to Frank, who asks Roberto to help compile it for presentation. Roberto looks at the data and is horrified. He realizes that submitting the circulation figures to Frank has put the jobs and schedules of most of his colleagues in jeopardy. He and Frank are working together, and there is no way for Roberto to hide the data or to present it in any other fashion. Personally, he wonders what has been going on in the other middle schools but keeps his comments to himself. He feels certain that if his data are included or considered to be the benchmark, then the other programs will be dramatically affected.

Questions

1. Are statistics such as Roberto's valid?
2. Should there be wide differences in this type of data for middle schools in the same city? Is it wise to compare middle schools from the same city with one another in this way?
3. What variables should be emphasized to allow for varying degrees of difference?
4. Why is Roberto's data set used as the benchmark?
5. What would be gained or lost by simply providing anecdotal data, instead of statistics, to try and save the programs and space?
6. Should Frank come up with another way to try and save the programs and space? What is Frank's role in all of this?
7. What other ways are there to combat the downsizing trend?
8. Is there any other way to explain the programs at the other schools so that the recipients of the data have a better perspective on their meaning?

7
Personnel

7.1. Quantum Leap—the Transfer from Elementary to Middle School

The transfer list for the Island Regional School Department is based on seniority. The list is carefully monitored, and certified employees wishing to transfer to another school within their same area of certification put their name on the list for that school. No interviews are conducted; seniority rules. When a vacancy occurs, the list is consulted and generally, when offered, the transfer takes place.

For those certified school library media specialists, the transfer process is a rather simple one. Since fixed schedules abound at the elementary level, most specialists are on the transfer list for any of the six high schools in the district, all of which have flexible schedules. Many of the middle school positions remain stable, as a large number of the district's school library media specialists dislike teaching students in those grades. The perception is that these are difficult years and it is easier to teach the very young or jump to the high school level. The incumbent middle school library media specialists feel that they have the best of all possible worlds—only a small percentage of fixed classes, team planning time to work on resource-based instruction and integrated units, and automated catalogs and access to many specialized resources. These eight school library media specialists are a close-knit group and feel collectively that a middle school is an enjoyable, challenging place for them.

Sally Jones and Maria Garcia are good friends. On Maria's advice, Sally has put her name on the transfer list to go to any middle school.

Sally has been at Peabody Valley Elementary for four years but is looking for a change. Maria has been at Norman Biddle Middle School for about the same time period. Maria feels that Sally would be a wonderful middle school library media specialist and has told her so. She feels that Sally's talents in curriculum and technology are lost within Peabody Valley's fixed schedule.

During the summer an opening occurs at Mountain Middle, and Sally is first on the transfer list. Sally accepts the position and calls Maria. Maria is euphoric. She is convinced that Sally will be very happy at Mountain Middle and that the district will benefit by having used Sally's strengths more effectively.

During a celebratory lunch the next day, the two women plan to visit Mountain Middle. Maria tells Sally that she will get the automated catalog up and running and will coach her through the system. With Sally's computer experience and knowledge, Maria is sure that one or two working sessions will be sufficient training for Sally.

Sally calls the principal at Mountain Middle, Penelope Peterson, and makes an appointment to meet her at 9 A.M. the following Monday. Maria then agrees to meet with Sally at 10:30 to visit Mountain Middle's library media center. Both will then work together at Mountain Middle for two days and then work together for two days at Norman Biddle. Maria figures that training starting now will help Sally to adjust to her new library media center before the start of school.

Since it is early August and school will not start until after Labor Day, there is plenty of time. Sally spends two days cleaning out at Peabody Valley and piles her car with her personal possessions—units she has developed, her laptop computer, posters that she's had autographed, and some stuffed animals.

At 10:30 on Monday, Maria pulls into the parking lot at Mountain Middle. Sally is standing next to her car crying in reaction to her conversation with the principal. Maria is beside herself when she hears what has taken place. Penelope has told Sally that she doesn't want someone at her school from an elementary school. Penelope wants a specialist in middle school librarianship and curriculum. She doesn't want just anybody—she wants a particular library media specialist who's already on the list and wants to transfer from another middle school to Mountain Middle School. Penelope wants Sally to call the Human Resources Department and decline the job offer so it will be given to the next person on the list, the one Penelope Peterson wants. Penelope told Sally not to go to the library media center or turn on any equipment, and she has instructed the head custodian not to give her keys to the room.

Maria tells Sally that Penelope has no grounds for the statements she has made. The agreement with the employees' bargaining unit makes the transfer situation clear, and the job is Sally's. Penelope thus has no grounds to make such demands. Maria convinces Sally to stand her ground and take the position. She tells her this will pass and together they go into the school to talk with Penelope.

Questions

1. Is Penelope's behavior professional?
2. What may be some consequences of this first meeting, should Sally decide to stay at Mountain Middle?
3. Is Sally's elementary school background relevant to the hiring decision?
4. Is Penelope's concern legitimate?
5. If the certification is for school library media specialist in grades K–12, does Penelope have any grounds to refuse Sally?
6. What rights does Sally have in this situation?
7. What is the role of the employees' bargaining unit in this case?
8. What is the role of the Human Resources Department?
9. Should the district supervisor have introduced Penelope to Sally?

7.2. Student Teacher Blues

Each semester Ramona Silvestri, library media specialist at Brightwood Junior High School, takes a practicum student from the library school at the university. Ramona is widely known for her dynamic programs, grant-writing skills, technology knowledge, and effervescent personality, and in the last nine years Ramona has supervised nearly fifteen future school library media specialists—all of whom have gotten jobs in their field and continue to consider her their mentor.

This semester Ramona has been approached by a number of library school students to serve as their supervisor during their practicum. As in the past, Ramona asks them to spend two full days at Brightwood's library media center. There they will see her in action, interacting with students and staff. They will also have the opportunity to help her with questions, routines of the day, supervising students, and so on. Ramona feels that when the students get this far in their program, the practicum experience simply pulls all of the pieces of their studies together into a working environment. Since her library media center is a one-person operation, she feels that personal dynamics are vital.

Bob Madden, a library school student, has approached Ramona about being a practicum candidate and spends two days at her school. Bob is quiet and has a distinctive speech impediment. Ramona has to concentrate to hear and understand what he is saying. Bob is content to listen to what Ramona says without offering any opinion. She shows him the facility and introduces him to the faculty, making a special effort to introduce him to the principal and his assistant. Bob has little, if anything, to say. Ramona asks him about his course work and what he's interested in doing when he finishes his MLS. She learns little about him, despite her questions. His career goals are vague; he's been out of work for several years and this is a career change for him. His emphasis, he tells Ramona, is just to get a job, any job.

During the second day of observation, a fight breaks out in the corridor just outside the library media center. Ramona goes out to assist. Two students, eighth-grade boys, are duking it out and a crowd has gathered. Ramona calls both of them by name, loudly enough to get their attention. She tells them to stop and puts her arms out to begin to separate them. Other teachers join in and the incident is over. Later, Bob tells Ramona that he doesn't know what he would do if confronted with such a situation. Ramona tells him that during their time together this is something they would work on. Bob takes Ramona's comments as a commitment from her to accept him as a practicum student. He is delighted and shows some real enthusiasm that Ramona hasn't seen before. Ramona isn't sure that she meant to take Bob, but given the awkwardness of the present situation, she confirms that she will work with him in the next semester.

Ramona sends Bob an outline of her expectations and speaks with him on the phone several times. She also speaks on the phone to the faculty member from the university who will be involved with Bob's practicum. Dr. Stephan Stokes, the instructor for the final practicum in the school library media program, is delighted that Ramona will be taking Bob under her wing. He confides in her that he's had some strong reservations about Bob's likelihood of success as a school library media specialist. Ramona is not happy to find out that Bob is such a marginal candidate. She shares this concern with Stephan and asks him to make more visits to her school during Bob's time there. Stephan agrees.

Bob's first day starts off poorly. He is two hours late and Ramona begins to think that either she's off on the day or he's been in a terrible accident. Bob shows up at ten o'clock saying that he didn't want to drive in the snowy weather and waited until the rush-hour traffic was over. He tells Ramona that he will make up the hours during the next two weeks. Ramona is flabbergasted, but she takes a deep breath and begins to show Bob how the on-line catalog works. She reviews with him the search procedures that she will use tomorrow with a class. He is to observe her first-period class; become actively involved with the second-period class (the same teacher is bringing all five sections of his eighth-grade American History students for a project on the Civil War); and, if he feels comfortable, take over period three. Ramona has prepared a bibliography, pulled books and magazines, identified sites on the Web, and met twice with the teacher.

Bob sits like a stone during the first class. His attempts to help during period two are rejected by the students, who look at him strangely, mimic his speech, and ask Ramona for help. Ramona glares at those doing the mimicry, but Bob seems oblivious. Bob rejects taking over period three and sits at a table for the remainder of the classes, making no attempt to assist or intervene. Ramona decides to talk with Bob after school about when he thinks he would like to begin to take a more active role with the students. She asks him to stay and talk with her and then leaves the room for a few minutes to go to the bathroom. On her way, she meets up with the American History teacher, who tells her she has her work cut out for her.

Questions

1. Is Bob's behavior just a result of his inexperience and natural timidity?
2. Is it likely that Bob will improve in time, given Ramona's expertise and mentoring?
3. What will Ramona need to do to help Bob improve?
4. What is the role of the college library school in preparing Bob for this practicum?
5. What did Bob accomplish to proceed this far in the library school program? Has there been some intervention by Dr. Stephan Stokes?

6. What should Ramona's first actions be when she meets with Bob to review the day?
7. Does Bob's speech impediment constitute a disability?
8. Should Bob have been guided to a less public type of library career?

7.3. Fair and Equitable or Just a Work Ethic Rewarded?

Samneth Chiu is the school library media specialist at the Thompson Valley Junior High School. She has been there for twelve years. Samneth is not active professionally; she has not joined the local or state professional associations, does not subscribe to professional journals, and rarely attends workshops or conferences.

Samneth is absent a significant amount of time. She suffers from migraines and takes off whenever she feels one coming on. Her principal has not been sympathetic and has written negative reports for chronic absenteeism several times. She uses all of her sick days each year, mostly on Mondays or Fridays. She is often late to school and has been reprimanded for this. Each time that her absenteeism or lateness has been documented in an effort to remove her, the principal has changed his mind and Samneth has continued her behavior. Exactly why he backed down is unclear. However, Samneth's district has not been successful in court when trying to get rid of employees, and perhaps the principal has been advised to work with or around Samneth.

Each day Samneth has a fixed schedule of four classes, in addition to one administrative period and one unassigned period. She has difficulty maintaining control of her four classes. The children just don't seem interested in her lessons on skills.

Samneth does only what is required, nothing more. She closes the library media center during her administrative period because she thinks that's when she is supposed to do clerical work, not circulate books or answer reference questions. During her unassigned period, Samneth is nowhere to be found. She has the right to leave the building during this time and almost always does. If the weather is bad and she stays in her room, the door is locked and no amount of knocking will bring her to answer it. The library media center at Thompson is rather dingy. No new posters have been hung; there's always tons of shelving to do; the books are everywhere in piles. Some of these need bar codes, some need labels, and some need repairs. There are no professional collection and no multimedia materials. Samneth says that there just isn't time in her schedule to handle everything, and she has to cover four classes.

Across town at the James Street Junior High, a new school library media specialist has been hired. Peter Abdullah transferred from an elementary school. The position was vacant for some time because James Street's library media center was a mess. Two years ago the library media specialist moved away and the next day a pipe burst in the room. There was quite a bit of damage. About one thousand books were destroyed; upholstered furniture was ruined along with the rug. The on-line catalog was disconnected and the substitutes didn't know how to get it running again. No one seemed interested in transferring there until this year. The district supervisor encouraged Peter to transfer to James Street and then arranged for him to have twenty days of pay during the summer in order to fix the center.

Peter transfers in January. He works long hours, repairs the shelves himself, replaces the furniture using donations, has the carpet cleaned using PTO funds, and hooks up the network and gets it going. Every day he does one thing that moves the library media center forward. He has a combination of both a fixed and flexible schedule, and after two weeks of laboring he begins to work cooperatively with teachers. By the Easter vacation, the principal is extolling his efforts citywide. The end-of-the-year meeting of the school library media specialists is held at James Street, and all of the other library media specialists are impressed. Samneth is totally surprised at the condition. Her building and James Street were built at the same time. Now, however, they look totally different. James Street is clean and bright with an air of purpose about it.

Samneth talks with Peter and discovers that he has twenty days over the summer to continue his renovation/restoration efforts. He tells her that in the fall his schedule will be completely flexible because the principal is impressed by what he has accomplished in such a short time. Samneth is furious.

Questions

1. Should Samneth also be eligible for twenty days of paid summer work?

2. Why does Peter Abdullah have the right to special privileges which the other library media specialists don't?
3. Is this a reward for Peter's ability to stay after and repair things, or is this a recognition of his professional efforts?
4. Is it fair and equitable that some junior high schools have fixed schedules while others have flexible ones?
5. Has the principal at Thompson Valley done a disservice to the district by not pursuing Samneth for disciplinary action?
6. What is the role of the school library media supervisor in this case?
7. Are the students at Thompson Valley receiving fair and equitable library services compared with those students at James Street?
8. How could Samneth be motivated to become a better employee?

7.4. The Revolving Clerk

Catholic Regional (known to students as "CR") is a new, regional parochial school housed in a new building but with faculty consolidated from a number of small junior high and middle schools that have been closed around the region. This is the first year that CR has been open, and the diocese has decided to spend time on faculty team building. The efforts include a week at a local seminar site where there will be speakers from around the state talking about middle school students and their special needs. The emphasis is on the faculty getting to know one another, getting to feel comfortable together, and building an organization that will be second to none. The traditional roles in the school are somewhat unusual for a modern-day school system. The faculty are put into teams consisting of four academic block subject teachers (math, science, language arts, and social science). Each team is responsible for managing their students. The rules are made up by the team and then enforced by them. There is no assistant principal at CR, nor is there a disciplinary prefect. The teams work together to educate the total child—academically and socially.

The other faculty at CR are also on a team. This team—consisting of the foreign language teachers, the health and physical education teachers, and the art, music, home economics, and computer teachers—is called the unified arts team. These teachers will work with the academic teams as their students leave the block team time to take advantage of electives. The unified arts teachers will plan class schedules after school with the academic teams and will have input into the concept of whole-child education.

The position of school library media specialist at CR is currently unfilled. There are a school library media center and many materials taken from the closed schools. There is one clerk who has been hired and worked all summer. Ms. Martinez is returning books to the shelves and plans to begin to put together an on-line catalog. The hardware and software have been purchased, and the computer records will be input over the coming year. The periodical subscriptions from the closed schools have been forwarded to CR, and new furniture has been purchased. Ms. Martinez was a clerk in the public library and is thrilled to work at CR because, as a benefit, her children can attend the school for free.

During the second week of school, a school library media specialist is hired. Ana Raposa has extensive experience in setting up new facilities and is hired for a five-year period. She is rather unorthodox in that she plans to quit at the end of her contract. She is in her mid-forties and has a private income. Ana wants to set up one more library media center before she quits and decided to take the job at CR because she believes in the importance of the educational experience for middle school students.

Ana speaks several languages and has lived abroad throughout parts of her life. She is married with grown children. She not only has an MLS but a doctor of arts (D.A.) in library administration. She is a take-charge person and wastes no time assigning a variety of tasks to Ms. Martinez. Ms. Martinez is happy working with Ana, and they both enjoy their new facility. At Christmas, however, Ms. Martinez's husband is transferred out of state and Ana must find a new clerk.

Ana, with the approval of the principal, places an ad in the local newspaper and calls several people she knows at temporary employment agencies. Although she wants someone full time, she will settle for someone for the semester. Ana interviews several candidates and selects Rosa Bernaly. Rosa shows up on time the first day but by ten o'clock she is in tears. She had no idea that she would be working so much with students. She is a whiz at word processing and has worked in one of the branches of the public library. She tells Ana tearfully that this just isn't her cup of tea. She leaves at noon and doesn't return. Ana then goes back to her file of applicants and calls Ruth Howard. Ruth comes in for a look at the job. She is wary because she was told the position was filled. Sure enough, she doesn't like what she sees. The money is not terrific, and the fringe benefit of free tuition is not a draw because Ruth has no children. The thought of spending the day with middle school or junior high school kids scares her to death. She sees them hanging out at the mall and just doesn't like them. She declines the position.

This scenario is repeated several more times with the person either quitting in a day or so or else being scared off by the students. Ana is now perplexed. She gets someone from a temporary agency to fill out the term and sits down to decide how to staff for the future.

Questions

1. Is there a problem between the perception and the reality of this clerical position?
2. What skills are needed for a clerical position in a school like CR?
3. What are these skills in priority order?
4. What is the difference between public library and school library clerical work?
5. Is the job description adequate? Should a new employee receive training similar to the faculty about working with middle school students?
6. Is training a parent to do the job a possibility?
7. Would there be issues of confidentiality if a parent worked at their child's school because of access to student records?

8
Resources and Equipment

8.1. Budgeting for School Reform

Nanette Malenkoff is principal of the Ezekiel Held Middle School in Princetown. Velma Grayson is the school's library media specialist. Nanette does not approve of the trend toward shared decision making. Her belief is that she is the principal and she runs the show. This has not always made for a harmonious relationship with the faculty and staff at Held.

Lately, the Princetown School Department has been working on school restructuring. To this end, each principal has been involved in training with shared decision making, organizational leadership, participatory management, and so on. Each principal has also been charged with developing a team at the school that will begin to take on decision-making roles in the area of curriculum and governance of the building. Nanette has participated in this training but doesn't want to do more than is essential to keep the Princetown School Department off her back. She feels that she is the educational leader for the school and that her vision is the school's vision. Velma, an avid reader, has stumbled upon some discussions of school reform in issues of *Educational Leadership* and also on LM_NET on the Internet. She researches this topic in various other journals and sources and comes to the conclusion that school reform and shared decision making are here to stay. She then surveys the collection at Ezekiel Held Middle School and comes to the realization that she doesn't have appropriate and relevant materials on this subject.

Velma's budget for the year is about $6 per child. There are seven hundred children enrolled at Held Middle School and this $4,200 must cover all print and nonprint materials, all journal subscriptions, and the consumable supplies (bar codes, copy paper, toner for the copier, and the like). In addition, it must also cover the service agreements for the online system. Velma has spent wisely in the past and created a balanced collection that meets the needs of the users. She has also been quite successful in raising additional monies through the PTO and local businesses for specific purchases.

Velma has no room in this year's budget for purchases other than those she has already identified. She plans ahead and commits all of her funds during the summer months so that materials arrive at the beginning of September. This year has been no exception. She might be able to raise additional money once the school year begins, but the funds would not be significant enough to develop a professional collection devoted to school reform issues. Velma also feels strongly that her library media center budget is already too small and her limited funds should not be diverted from those materials directly related to the students and the curriculum. Velma decides to enlist Nanette's help.

Velma and Nanette arrived at Held together. They are about the same age and enjoy a mutual respect. Both are avid bridge players and enjoy golfing, although they have never played together. Velma stops by school and offers to take Nanette to lunch, something she has done in the past with no hidden agenda. During lunch she and Nanette discuss the summer program for administrators that Nanette has just completed. Velma listens as Nanette talks about her vision for the future of Ezekiel Held Middle School and finds herself wondering if the faculty and parents share or are even aware of this vision. During the conversation Velma mentions that, given the present trends in site-based management, central administration must have certain expectations of the Held School, expectations that the library resources should help the faculty fulfill.

Nanette remains unconvinced that this is something that the library staff needs to worry about but does finally agree to free up $200 from her principal's budget so that Velma can buy a few books on site-based management for the teachers. As lunch ends, Nanette suggests some titles that she has seen in the local bookstore. She encourages Velma to get some requisitions together and buy these items. She cautions her, however, that site-based management is another passing fancy and she should reserve her library media center budget for issues that are here to stay. Velma is aware of the titles that Nanette has suggested and doesn't feel that they are adequate to educate the teachers on the topic of school reform. The books Nanette has suggested deal with specifics of thematic units, grant writing, discipline, and scheduling.

Questions

1. Was Velma correct in inviting Nanette to lunch?
2. Did Velma have a hidden agenda, and was a lunch setting an appropriate place to address it?
3. Is the principal correct in saying that the library media center doesn't need to worry about this passing trend?
4. Do the library media specialist and the library media center have to support every faculty trend?
5. To what extent should Velma's budget support this effort?
6. Should Velma appeal directly to the school department for financial support so she can add this emphasis to the collection?
7. Does Nanette's support from her own principal's budget indicate fundamental support for school reform?

8.2. Circulation of Computers

Mary Grace West is an experienced middle school library media specialist. She has been at Nathanielson Middle School for a number of years. During that time she has turned the library media center around. Active professionally, she visits other sites, confers with colleagues, reads voraciously, and writes grants for everything from book jackets to furniture. The collection is well used and the faculty support her efforts enthusiastically.

Last year at a conference, Mary Grace saw a vendor promoting small laptop computers. These machines weighed about four pounds and were really glorified word processors. They had 64 kilobytes of memory, had spell check and thesaurus features, and could print to both Macintosh and IBM printers. The machines had a twelve-hour battery and were stored in a charging unit about the size of one of her library tables. Each charging unit held thirty to thirty-five machines. Mary Grace was impressed with what she saw as the possibilities for such a machine. She spoke with the vendor and then collected as much literature about the product as possible. Upon her return to Nathanielson she stored this data in her "wish file."

About three months later Mary Grace saw a request for proposal (RFP) in a grants alert newsletter. The granting agency was interested in funding hardware acquisitions by urban schools serving students in grades 5 through 8. The agency felt that the technology gap between urban and suburban school children in these grades was significant and in years to come would widen even more. Mary Grace remembered the little laptops that she had seen at the conference and pulled out the documentation.

Mary Grace had a template of facts about her school stored in her computer. She pulled it up, rechecked the RFP, and began to write. She envisioned two units in the library media center, each holding about thirty laptops. The storage units had built-in locks and just needed access to a plug to recharge the individual laptops. Printers were already available in the library media center. Mary Grace thought that giving the students access to the laptops for writing school papers would help them in a variety of ways. Full of enthusiasm, Mary Grace wrote and wrote. When she took the grant to the principal, Mr. Alvarez, for his endorsement he was as enthusiastic as she was. Technologically adept, Mr. Alvarez was an enthusiastic supporter of any of Mary Grace's grant-writing efforts. He too shared her vision of laptops in the library media center.

As they continued to discuss the RFP, it became clear that Mary Grace wanted to circulate the laptops while Mr. Alvarez wanted them available in the library for use. Mary Grace pulled out her documentation regarding the technology gap between urban and suburban students and focused on the absence of technology as a major factor for urban students. By letting the laptops circulate, she reasoned, the entire family would have access to them. Parents, siblings, and the like would see the student using the laptop for an assignment. They too could learn about the uses of the computer and the computer literacy levels of all would be raised. Mary Grace explained to Mr. Alvarez that she would put bar code numbers on the laptops and circulate them for three days at a time. Students and their parents would be required to sign out the machines, agreeing to be responsible for loss or damage. Furthermore, parents would have to pick up the machines themselves on behalf of their child. This, Mary Grace reasoned, would bring more parents into the school. A one-hour demonstration course would be offered, and only students who had successfully completed the course would be permitted to take out the laptops. Mr. Alvarez was not convinced that lending computers was the responsibility of either the library media center or the library media specialist. He was also concerned about who would conduct this training and how issues of damage or loss would be handled. He signed the grant but told Mary Grace that they had much to discuss.

Questions

1. Is lending laptops a responsibility that should be adopted by a library media center?
2. Is Mary Grace the appropriate member of the faculty or administration to be writing grants for this type of equipment?
3. Who will teach the demonstration course? Who will train that person?
4. Should Mary Grace have written this grant without first clearing it with the principal?
5. How should Mary Grace approach the circulation question with Mr. Alvarez? What policies could be implemented to improve the circulation of the laptops?
6. What guidelines should the district and Nathanielson Middle School impose for grant writing?
7. Should teachers be free to write grants on their own, regardless of the effect the funds and their use will have on the school?
8. Should the district or the school have a technology committee to standardize hardware acquisitions?
9. Should the district or the school have a technology plan?
10. Would lending laptops through the library media center fit into this plan?

8.3. Time to Move: What Do We Keep? How Do We Pay for Replacements?

Curriculums, teachers, and administrators have come and gone at Western Junior High School. Tomas Jimenez has lived through many changes in his twenty-plus years there and hopes to retire soon. He is a fixture at Western and is now teaching the children of the children he taught his first year. Tomas began his teaching career as a reading teacher and then earned an MLS at the university. He went to school at night for five years to earn his degree and then had to wait another five years before the school library media specialist position was available. Other positions in other buildings came and went, but Tomas wanted to remain at Western Junior High School.

At one time Western Junior High housed grades 7 through 9 and at another time grades 5 through 8. Most recently it has been home to 750 students in grades 7 and 8. Now, the latest population shifts have created large class sizes at the lower grades, squeezing some fifth and sixth graders out of their traditional schools and into Western. The senior high school in the district is quite large, and the seventh and eighth grades are going there in the fall. The new configuration at Western will be about 600 fifth and sixth graders—including special education, gifted, ESL, and bilingual Spanish. The new name of the school will be Western Transitional School. The school will offer the typical fifth- and sixth-grade curriculums with students changing classes and leaving their grade and homeroom for electives such as home economics, shop, and art. The flexible library program that was so effective with grades 7 and 8 will continue for the students at Western School. Tomas will continue to work on resource-based instruction with the school's teachers and hopes to get them to think in terms of themes for the first year. He hopes the themes will focus on the transitional concept that is integral to the school.

Tomas has been hired for the summer to select books that will be sent to the high school and to build a collection for the transitional students. There is a statewide funding formula that is used for the new transitional collection. Given the lower grade levels and thus lower reading levels, Tomas will have to identify fiction and nonfiction titles that will be appropriate for both informational and recreational reading. Tomas initially finds it easy to identify books to ship to the high school. Most of the older fiction will go, giving him adequate shelf space for titles he will identify for his new students. As he pulls the books and deletes them out of the on-line catalog, however, Tomas wonders about the value of some of these titles. Sure, they are well written and by writers of repute. They have even won awards. The focus of the curriculum, however, has changed since these titles were acquired. They've sat on the shelves for five years and not circulated. Tomas is a bit embarrassed that he didn't weed them out before this. Now he questions whether or not to ship them over to the high school.

Tomas contacts Georgia Petra, the library media specialist at Western Senior High School. Georgia, like Tomas, has been hired to facilitate the move by weeding her existing collection to make room for the titles she'll be adding—the titles Tomas will be shipping over. The two of them meet at Tomas's library media center to discuss strategy. Georgia brings some reading lists that she's prepared with the English and social studies teachers. She also brings some themes that she knows will be used in some of the new eleventh- and eighth-grade classes in the fall. Together she and Tomas realize that just shifting books from one school to another is not the answer. They both feel that funds are needed above and beyond what is already budgeted. These funds would support new reading initiatives and allow for greater resource-based instruction efforts. As Tomas and Georgia work, Tomas realizes that he has been negligent in the last several years by not weeding aggressively and not being more forceful in getting more funds to keep the collection up to date. He has relied heavily on cooperation with the local public library and interlibrary loan from other libraries and has failed to keep his collection current. He has mapped the collection but only when glaring errors and omissions were identified. Now he and Georgia must go to the high school principal and the district supervisor to gain support for updating the collection instead of just moving it.

Questions

1. What are some early warning signs that could have alerted Tomas to his increasingly out-of-date collection?
2. What could have been done before Tomas and Georgia were hired for the summer to shift the seventh- and eighth-grade titles?
3. What should Tomas do to avoid this type of situation in the future?
4. How long should quality fiction sit on the shelf once its circulation decreases and it no longer meets the needs of the school curriculum?
5. Should there be a collection policy in place for all grade levels/school levels that would be specific enough to cover this type of situation?
6. How should Georgia and Tomas approach the principal and district supervisor so that the problem is solved without pointing fingers and assigning blame?

8.4. Encyclopedia Acquisitions: Paper or CD? Both Types or One?

The St. Agatha School is one of the most prestigious in the diocese of Benningville. It offers young men and women a rigorous academic environment for grades 6 through 8. The school's philosophy emphasizes excellence through diversity. Most of the graduates go on to prestigious preparatory schools, both parochial and private.

Situated in a fashionable area of Benningville, the campus consists of three buildings—one for academics, one for sports, and one for the library. Enrollment is by interview and test. The students pay what they can and no one is denied admission because of finances. This blind policy about need has allowed academically talented youngsters to study in a conducive atmosphere. The graduates are most generous and have continued to underwrite the school's finances over the last seventy-five years.

Brother Andrew Chan is the library media specialist at St. Agatha. He is quite a go-getter and considered a "librarian's librarian." He has weathered the change from the traditional view of library media centers and library media specialists and is just as comfortable with resource-based instruction, information literacy, on-line catalogs, CD products, and the like as he ever was with the Dewey Decimal System and the Anglo-American Cataloging Rules. Brother Andrew keeps up professionally, is a frequent speaker at professional meetings, and has written several articles showcasing St. Agatha's School library media center.

Last year, St. Agatha's was selected to participate in a test for a large software company. The Software Connection is a leading manufacturer of educational CD-ROM products. They have found their marketing niche by focusing on families and schools and creating a quality product. Their product line includes encyclopedias, atlases, almanacs, and dictionaries, all on CD-ROM. Additionally, they sell biographical CDs, animal CDs, CDs focusing on various time periods in history, and so on. Their product line is diversified and growing. Brother Andrew had used several of Software Connection's products at St. Agatha's before the school was selected as a test site for new products. Now, each month he gets at least one new CD and is required only to keep a log about its use and effectiveness.

The library media center at St. Agatha's has several rooms. There is a reading room, a periodical room, a reference room, the open-stack area, a large lobby that houses the circulation desk, some exhibit space, and a computer room. The computer room houses all of the computers for the school. There are both IBM and Macintosh machines and plenty of space for two classes to use the room simultaneously. In addition to Brother Andrew there is a reference librarian, a computer teacher, a circulation technician, a cataloger, and a cataloging technician. The cataloger does acquisitions and collection development, as most of the titles are purchased with MicroLif data and bar code numbers. The budget for print materials is $20,000, and the collection consists of 15,000 volumes. The library's schedule is open and flexible. It is open daily from 7 A.M. until 10 P.M., Monday through Friday, and 1–6 P.M. on Saturday and Sunday. Recently, Brother Andrew and Belinda Johnson, the cataloger, have been looking closely at the reference collection. The encyclopedias are scheduled for updating, and they disagree on how this is to be done. Brother Andrew figures that with four IBM and four Macintosh CD workstations, a close review of the reference collection is certainly warranted. The paper (print) encyclopedias are five years old. With four different CD encyclopedias (in both IBM and Mac format), why should the paper (print) ones be replaced? Also, what about some of the more specialized encyclopedias? If there are eight workstations (not networked) for running the CD products and the CDs are available in both formats, why spend $300–$500 replacing paper (print) editions? Since the partnership with the Software Connection sends so many CD products to the school for free, why not expand and update the reference tools in CD format?

Ms. Johnson, who occasionally works on weekends, has some data about waiting queues of students who want to use the biographical CDs and the general encyclopedic ones. She has found it necessary to limit the time at the workstations on Saturdays. Furthermore, she often finds herself just printing off the appropriate article and giving it to the student to minimize the waiting time. In many cases she finds herself making the decision about what article is appropriate for the reference query. This, she says, is not teaching the student about research and on-line search strategies. It does, however, give the student the material, but she has done all of their research work.

Brother Andrew and Ms. Johnson have worked together for many years. They have a great deal of mutual respect for one another, both personally and professionally. Rather than make a hasty decision, they agree to maintain their respective positions (Brother Andrew for CD format and Ms. Johnson for print) and meet again in four weeks. During that time each will research this topic and provide both statistical and anecdotal information to support their positions.

Questions

1. Should the library media center maintain both paper (print) and CD versions of encyclopedias?
2. If the CD versions are free because the school is part of the marketing test, does it matter if budgeted funds are spent on paper (print) editions?
3. Would the queuing time be less if the stations were networked?
4. What is the value of having CD stand-alone workstations versus networked ones?
5. The marketing test won't last forever; when should St. Agatha's build a budget line for software?
6. What kind of statistical data should Brother Andrew and Ms. Johnson gather to support their respective positions?
7. What kind of anecdotal data should they gather?

9
Facilities

9.1. Equipment That Keeps On Ticking

The library media center at the Island Middle School was once state of the art. Island was the first in the district to have an on-line catalog. Their library media center was on the map because of technological advances. As an urban middle school this set Island apart and the library media specialist, Mark Davidoff, made a name for himself around the region. He spoke to groups of principals and teachers on the way instruction changes when technology is involved. He spoke to library media specialists about how to go from a nineteenth- to a twenty-first-century library media center in one year. Mark was a good speaker, and people listened. He set the benchmark, but then something happened.

Mark spent so much time telling other people how to get started and helping his colleagues in the district write plans, write grants, and then implement those technology plans that he neglected his own center. The system that Mark worked with in 1992 consisted of seven IBM 286 machines networked for searching and circulation. The six small machines that served as circulation or search stations were controlled by a 286 with an expanded hard drive. Mark also had four IBM 386 machines with CD-ROM drives. He ran Windows 3.1 on those. One of these 386 machines had Internet capability. Finally, he had an Apple IIc that he used for general word processing and for making signs with PrintShop software. He also had some interesting classroom programs for this machine.

Now, Mark finds himself running ragged trying to coax the network into action each day. He runs the search and circulation stations from disks that access the network and constantly has to scrounge for parts.

Behind the circulation desk there is a jumble of wires, cables, and so on—a hazard that Mark knows only too well, having slipped several times and pulled out a connection. The network, even when it is running, is often slow, and the students grow impatient as they wait for access.

The four CD-ROM workstations are hardly state of the art. Many of the newer CDs need more RAM and run better in a 3.11 or Windows 95 environment. The graphics are slow and the printers don't do them justice. Mark has lots of disk-based programs about health and science for the Apple IIc, and while they're valuable, they take too much time to operate.

Mark realizes that his equipment needs to be upgraded but he consoles himself with the fact that it works and does the job, although not consistently and not efficiently. Mark is so busy trying to hold his system together that he has little opportunity to plan for an upgrade. He knows that some library media centers are involved in upgrading their technology and he takes some comfort in having been the spark that ignited their interest. However, he feels that he will hold the present system together for one or two more years and then approach the district supervisor with an eye to upgrading it.

Across town, Nancy Choi has been planning for technology for years. She has had small successes such as an IBM 486 that she bought with money raised by a book fair. Several IBM 386 machines have expanded capability and are used in the library media center with some CD products and Windows 95. She goes to conferences and offers to test new products, and with her mix of students and faculty many companies latch onto her. Nancy and a group of teachers and parents have formed a technology committee. This committee meets quarterly with an eye to reviewing hardware and software donations coming into the building. Nancy chairs the committee, whose goal is to have some standardization across equipment. Several years ago, the committee decided to purchase or accept as gifts only IBM or compatible machinery. They felt that this would allow for consistency in training, applications, and ease of use. By having the same type of hardware, the committee thought the faculty would develop more facility with it and use the equipment more often and more appropriately. The equipment is scattered throughout the school so students can receive word processing and computer-assisted instruction. These are mostly IBM 286 machines that run Professional Write. In the library, however, the 486 runs CDs and is connected to a bubble jet printer. On the 486 Nancy has loaded WordPerfect, Word, Professional Write, and Works. With the high-quality printer, documents that are generated in the classrooms can be printed in house with quality results.

Nancy has been advised that there is $30,000 available through the district for technology. The monies will be awarded based upon a plan for use. Nancy decides to apply and gathers her committee to write a proposal. Their emphasis is to completely upgrade the library media center's operation by having both an on-line network and several networked CD workstations. The existing library computers will be farmed out to the classrooms, while machines with quad-speed CD-ROMs and one gigabyte of RAM will be housed in the library. With the ever-dropping prices of hardware, the technology committee feels that they should be able to maximize their dollars and put the library media center on the map.

Questions

1. What are the strengths and weaknesses of the approaches used by Nancy and Mark?
2. Mark's network is still functioning, so is there any risk in waiting another year or so to upgrade?
3. With the dropping prices of some hardware, should Nancy and her committee wait another year to see if they can get more for their money?
4. Why does Nancy head the technology committee and not the business teacher or the principal?
5. Why should Mark's school have a technology committee and a purchase plan?
6. Does the district have a master plan for technology? If so, how does Nancy's plan mesh with it?
7. Are there additional sources of funding so that more than one school can be automated?

9.2. Partnership with Strings

The MicroMacro World Company is a leading manufacturer of computer software for library media centers. The company is headquartered in Dexter Center and it is a good neighbor to the community. Each year, the company donates hardware and software to various local schools. It asks only that publicity shots be permitted to publicize the donations. Each time a computer program, new printer, or scanner is donated to one of Dexter Center's schools, there are photo opportunities that are covered by the local media. No one from the company ever comes in to ask who is using what's been donated or how. No one worries about compatibility of hardware or usefulness of software. All of the equipment is clean, in working order, and in greater quantity than any Dexter Center school could ever afford.

This year Marco Merceau, the district library media supervisor, receives a phone call from the community relations office at MicroMacro World. The company would like to donate an entire network to one of the middle school library media centers in Dexter Center. They propose a Novell Network for circulation and searching with about ten workstations attached to a server. All hardware will be new and the software will be a product that is currently under development by MicroMacro World. The circulation/search software is so new that it will be tested at the selected middle school and then marketed nationally. MicroMacro World is breaking into the library systems market and wants a showplace for its products. Its circulation and search software will be aggressively marketed and it is anxious to capture a large share of the small academic and public library market. It may also market the system to special-interest libraries.

Marco tells MicroMacro World that he needs to see its proposal in writing and then would like to meet with a representative while a site is selected. Marco feels that this is a golden opportunity to reward one of the middle schools and to garner enough support within the Dexter Center School Department to automate the other library media centers when the product reaches the marketplace.

When the proposal arrives, Marco is disturbed to find out that MicroMacro will not only donate the hardware and software, set it up, train the staff, and maintain it but also monitor its use by patrons. Marco realizes that part of the development efforts that the company will test for involve tracking how users access the database, the problems that arise, the effects of various search strategies, and so on. Each child and teacher in the database will have their complete circulation records stored on the server and downloaded regularly by MicroMacro. The search portion of the program requires the user to use their name when accessing the print and nonprint resources. MicroMacro wants this information for strategic planning and product development. The final version of the software will not include these tracking features. As a reward for participating in the test, the selected middle school not only is allowed to keep the networked hardware and the final tested software but also will receive one year of free maintenance.

Marco decides that this is the only way he can bring one of his library media centers into the twenty-first century. He writes to the five middle school library media specialists and spells out the exact terms of the MicroMacro offer. He makes no judgments, but simply asks the library media specialists to join him in his office the following Friday to discuss which of the schools will be selected.

Questions

1. What criteria should be used for selecting the site for the test?
2. Should the users at that site be informed that their library usage is being monitored?
3. Are there other ways of studying the use of the system without violating people's right to privacy? Could the records be accessed without the users' names?
4. Is there a districtwide policy concerning gifts?
5. Does the district have guidelines regarding testing of hardware and software for commercial vendors?
6. If the chosen site needs an updated electrical system to run the network, who will pay for it?
7. If new furniture is required to hold all of this hardware, who will pay for it?
8. What are the long-term implications for the district and the school for maintaining this system?

9.3. The Overage Room, Formerly the Library Media Center

Jovanny Morales is furious. As the school's library media specialist, he's come back to school during August to hang up new posters, check on the order for new books, see about some equipment sent out for repairs, and just look the place over. He generally works half days during the last three weeks of August to prepare things for the start of school. When he opened the door this morning he could not believe the disarray. The equipment and tables and map cases have been moved around in the library media center, and ten new student desks and a free-standing blackboard have been added. He immediately seeks out Karl Paulus, the head custodian. Karl has been at Hilltop Junior High School for about fifteen years. He and Jovanny came at about the same time. Both men enjoy hockey and often chat about their favorite teams. Karl comes down the hall to the library media center with a frown on his face. His face and body language indicate his discomfort with Jovanny's presence in the library media center. He tells Jovanny that there are changes to be made for the fall semester and that Jovanny should see the principal. Jovanny, still seething, asks Karl to explain what has happened. Karl just shrugs his shoulders and walks away.

Jovanny barges into principal Cynthia Washington's office and demands to know what kind of junk is stored in his room and whose idea it was to put it there. Cynthia shoots back that Jovanny should calm down and she'll explain the situation. Jovanny tells her he's going down to the coffee machine and will be back shortly. He warns her that the story had better be good.

When Cynthia and Jovanny finally sit down to talk, Jovanny learns nothing new, only a new spin on an old story. For several years now increasing enrollments have swelled class sizes in the elementary schools. The crest of the wave has just hit seventh grade and there is not a seat to be had. Cynthia tells Jovanny that this year the enrollment at Hilltop is so great that she needs two new classrooms. She decided to close the library media center for part of each day and use the space for much needed classrooms. There are temporary partitions coming in and each half of the library media center will accommodate twenty-five students. Classes in the library will have their academic courses in the morning on Monday, Wednesday, and Friday and in the afternoon on Tuesday and Thursday. When they are not with their academic subject teachers, the students will be in electives, lunch, or gym and the library media center will be open for regular business on those days and at those times.

Cynthia tells Jovanny that this is what is going to happen for the remainder of the year. He can get used to it or he can fight her daily on this and lose. She feels that with Karl's help, each day when the students leave their classroom in the library media center, the desks and blackboard can be shoved against the wall and generally put out of the way.

Then, the library media center will be transformed back to its original purpose. This is a one-year plan only, Cynthia assures Jovanny, as portable classrooms will be installed the next summer to handle the groundswell of students hitting the junior high schools.

Jovanny says nothing. He likes and respects Cynthia. She has a tough job managing this expanding junior high school and does the job well. He knows that the exploding temper tantrum he had earlier is forgotten and that now the two of them have to work around this new configuration. He is puzzled, however, that Cynthia has decided to convert the library media center and not some other space such as the art room or music room. He tells her he is still in shock and will go home to think about the situation and what his response will be.

Questions

1. Why did the principal choose the library media center instead of the art room or the music room?
2. Why was Jovanny not involved in the decision-making process?
3. With classrooms of students in the room, will equipment get vandalized or stolen? How will the books on the shelves be affected?
4. Will this situation work?
5. What can or should Jovanny do?
6. Can classes and library services be offered in the center at the same time?
7. Should Jovanny set up a minicollection somewhere else in the school and just give the library media center over to a classroom for this one year?
8. What is the principal's perception of the library media center and its programs if she is prepared to take this type of action?
9. Are there state or local standards in effect that require physical access to the library media center and its collections?
10. Does the library have to be in the library media center? With an online network and CD products and the Internet, is the library media center portable?

9.4. The Library Media Center As a Coffee House

It is 7:15 A.M. and Lori Schultz has just opened the doors to the library media center. She's got the network up and running and has put the two daily newspapers on the room's coffee table in the lounge area. Over on the instructional side, she's placed a thermos of coffee on a small tray with some paper cups. She grabs the latest edition of *Teacher Magazine* and puts it next to the thermos. She stands back and surveys her domain—the flowers on the windowsill need watering and she hurries off to do this.

This scene is repeated on a regular basis throughout the school year at the Laurel Lake Middle School. Located in the quiet community of Laketon, Laurel Lake has an enrollment of nine hundred students in grades 5 through 9. It has a library media center that is the size of three normal classrooms. While not new, the furniture is in good condition, and there's an up-to-date fiction and nonfiction collection and an on-line catalog to access this collection. Lori, the school's library media specialist, has worked hard to keep the technology current but equally hard to keep the print resources current as well.

Each year, Laurel Lake surpasses the other schools in the district in terms of circulation and use for reference purposes. The library media center is at the center of the school's activities, the hub of the learning wheel. Lori feels that much of this perception of the role of the library media center is due to her personal understanding of the importance of the center.

Lori feels that the library media center should be warm and inviting and to that end she has divided the room into two sections. There is no wall but rather a sense that one side (with traditional tables and chairs) is for group instruction, while the other side (with several lounge chairs, a couch, a coffee table, etc.) is for less formal use. There is an area for supplies; the tape dispensers, paper cutter, staplers, and scissors are kept handy. There is always music playing—something soft and soothing. The place is alive and actually jumping by 7:30 each morning and again at the end of the day.

Teachers congregate in the room to look at the paper, chat, and have coffee. The students come in for personal recreational reading, to find homework help, and just to chat. The students notice the regular presence of the coffee thermos and the congregation of teachers around it. Some of them tease Lori by saying they want to have a cup.

In November the president of the Laurel Lake Student Council asks to see Lori after school. When they meet, he informs her that a petition has been passed asking for student access to coffee in the library media center before school. The PTO has agreed to pay for the supplies, and the students are eager to begin enjoying this privilege. Lori is taken aback. She feels that having student access to drink in the library media center will open a whole host of problems—spills, furniture damage, bugs, clean up, and so on. She also feels that coffee is only the beginning. Can Danish and croissants be far behind? What will they want next—an espresso or hot chocolate machine?

Lori talks with the principal and the district library media supervisor. Both tell her that the decision is hers, that the space and furniture are her responsibility and she must feel comfortable with her decision. Lori begins to wonder about letting the faculty drink in the library media center. She's not sure how all of this got started and now it seems to be getting out of hand. Because of the presence of the coffee and the newspaper, the teachers congregate in the library media center. This gives Lori the opportunity to talk with them about their classes, her programs, and the like. It has helped tremendously with her circulation. She wonders what will happen if the coffee program stops. But in her heart of hearts she just doesn't want to become the manager of the Laurel Lake School coffee house.

Questions

1. Is there a district policy on food and drink in rooms with furniture and equipment like that in the library media center?
2. How and why did this social situation get started?
3. Is there a trade-off here? By keeping the coffee does Lori keep her students and teachers in the library media center as active users?
4. Who will maintain this new expanded coffee program? Who will clean up? Who will buy the supplies?
5. What kinds of problems arise when there are drinks available in a library media center? Have teachers damaged any books or other contents in the center to date?
6. If drinks are available today, will food be far behind?

7. If coffee is served before school, will this lead to users wanting something served after school? When does the coffee stop or is it served all day?
8. What does this role of coffee maker do to Lori's image as the library media specialist?
9. Can and should Lori restrict where the coffee can be drunk to minimize damage to equipment and furniture? Is this a control issue?

10
District, Regional, and State Leadership

10.1. Who's in Charge Here?

Barry Dexter is the director of the Fund for Library Improvement. This is a grant position that operates out of the local business chamber. The business chamber sought out the funding from a number of national grant agencies. The focus of the grant is to improve library services in the schools of Plain City. Plain City is a large, urban area with twenty-two elementary and eight middle schools, as well as several high schools. The libraries are underfunded and understaffed, and, with their fixed schedule of classes, act as holding tanks for their respective schools. The Fund for Library Improvement seeks to bring about change through partnerships with the business community, increased funding, resource-based instruction, and a host of other initiatives.

Barry is a former library media specialist with about twelve years of experience. He has also worked in several small public libraries and done some part-time reference work at the local college. He is active professionally, serving at the regional and national level of the American Library Association. Barry is well organized and has a lot of contacts throughout the library profession. It is this bank of contacts along with his strong interview that got him the position with the business chamber.

As the director of the Fund for Library Improvement, Barry is responsible for monitoring grant monies of nearly $2 million. His specific charge is to use that money to bring about reform in the decaying urban library environment in Plain City. He reports to the business chamber executive director and has his own advisory board. This advisory board is composed of library and business leaders, as well as the assistant superintendent of Plain City and the district library supervisor.

Barry is a take-charge person who met with the district supervisor as soon as he took over. Together they began to formulate a plan for implementing some of the changes that the grant seeks to bring about. Barry's focus is on training the library media specialists for flexible scheduling and for book selection to meet the demands of resource-based instruction. He also wants a training program that will refocus administrators' scheduling priorities so the library media center will no longer be used as a holding tank for students during teachers' unassigned periods. Furthermore, Barry wants to bring in consultants both to help redesign the physical space in each library media center and to advise on how to implement technology.

Barry and the district supervisor, Kathy Sadler, do not get off to a good start. Barry has made no attempt to hide his lack of respect for Kathy because she is not a library media specialist. Kathy has been a reading teacher, a guidance counselor, and an assistant principal in several middle schools. She is bright, does her homework, and is enthusiastic about the Fund for Library Improvement's plan to bring about reform. She was one of the key people in writing the initial proposal and sits on Barry's advisory board.

Although she finds Barry's style a bit abrupt, she is willing to overlook it in order to bring about the changes she feels are so necessary. At the first meeting of library media specialists, Kathy introduces Barry and explains about the grant. Barry presents his plans for training, for outside consultants, and the like. He makes a few disparaging remarks about the administrators in Plain City and refers to them collectively as "the suits." The assembled library media specialists are uneasy. Although Kathy is often unable to deliver on her promises of more funding and staffing, she is easy to work with and always willing to listen. Some like Barry's take-charge attitude and the significant changes he represents. They feel that the only hope for change is from outside of the Plain City system.

At future meetings, both formal and informal, the clash of styles and personalities becomes more apparent. The library media specialists are split: Many look to Barry to solve problems that are building related; others expect Kathy to take more of an active role in the grant and less of an advisory one. Many of the younger and less experienced library media specialists begin to look to Barry as the supervisor. They feel that he can relate more to their issues, as he's been a library media specialist with a fixed schedule and too little funding. At the end of the first quarter of the grant operation, Kathy falls and breaks her knee and ankle. She is out of work for three months and Barry begins to make significant inroads into the day-to-day management of the Plain City library media centers.

Questions

1. Is there anything wrong with Barry assuming some of Kathy's responsibilities in her absence?
2. Is there an overlap between Barry's responsibilities and those of the district supervisor?
3. How are their responsibilities different, and how are they the same?
4. Should Barry's efforts in the day-to-day operations of library media centers in Plain City be curtailed? By whom?
5. How much of this is caused by Kathy's lack of formal library training and how much by personality?
6. Are the younger staff members swayed by Barry's funding, or do they really feel that he is more able to help them than Kathy?
7. What will happen when Kathy returns?
8. What is the role of the business chamber in all of this?
9. What is the role of the Fund for Library Improvement's advisory board?

10.2. I'm a BRIGHT Teacher, Are You?

For the last four summers the state university has offered training in computer technology to teachers and administrators. Specifically, this training has focused on ways to incorporate the Internet and e-mail into the traditional classroom. Each school in the Gotham Heights School District was encouraged to send teams of teachers to the training program called BRIGHT—Bringing Reform Into Gotham Heights Teaching. A team from each school received a PC, a designated line for Internet use, the opportunity to create a Web site for their school, fifteen hours of training, and software needed to connect to the local school network. Each summer, more and more teachers have taken advantage of the

BRIGHT training. About 100 teachers from Gotham Heights, all math or science certified, have completed the program and begun to use the PC in their classroom. Students can now search the Internet for information and e-mail their friends and pen pals.

The library media specialists at Gotham Heights have lobbied the state university for the last three summers to be permitted to take advantage of this training. They feel that as navigators of the information highway they are in the primary position to provide training in search strategies, advise about classroom integration of new technologies, and recommend hardware and software. Currently, the state university is considering admitting some school library media specialists into the BRIGHT program next summer.

This past summer, Betsy Carlson took the BRIGHT training. She is the library media specialist at the Gotham Heights Magnet Middle School. To teach at this school each teacher must have dual certification and Betsy's second certification is in math. In this capacity, she was admitted to the BRIGHT program and completed the training. Because she is also a school library media specialist, she has gotten herself appointed by the district supervisor as the technology liaison. Betsy has been released from all of her responsibilities at Magnet Middle to hook up hardware and software at all of the other Gotham Heights middle schools. She sets up e-mail accounts for faculty, provides training for the school library media specialist, and serves as an internal consultant on the Internet for the Gotham Heights School District.

Martha Perry is the school library media specialist at Benchly Middle School. Martha has not yet taken the BRIGHT training but has a master of business adminstration degree (MBA) along with her MLS. She is certified as both a school library media specialist and a computer teacher at the secondary level. Martha feels that the BRIGHT training is just a way to get a free PC. She finds that teachers at her school do very little in the classrooms about teaching students to use search strategies. She does not think teachers connect the technology to their regular lessons. Most of the students know a few Web sites (nba.com, concerning basketball, is the principal one) and the teachers seem just to enjoy conversing with other teachers on the Net. Martha has ten computers in the library media center. Six of the computers operate her on-line catalog, while the remaining four are stand-alone CD-ROM workstations with Internet capability. She teaches the students and teachers in her building about searching the Internet, creating bookmarks to mark their favorite Web sites, using e-mail, and installing hardware and software. She has created a home page for her school and another one for just her library media center.

Martha and Betsy are friends, but Martha resents that Betsy is now considered the technology liaison. She feels that one summer of training doesn't begin to compensate for an MBA, computer certification, and hands-on experience with software evaluation and installation. Martha begins to recommend that teachers in her building establish e-mail accounts. From a BRIGHT-trained teacher, she gets the address for activating new accounts and handles that for her building. She also obtains a copy of Netscape 3.0, which she proceeds to load into all of the PCs in the building. She then notifies the principal that she will be available to provide training at her school for Internet and e-mail functions. Her justification is that she is only doing this for her building. Since Betsy is handling all of the other schools, this will limit the need for her services in Martha's building.

Questions

1. What are the ethical questions involved in Martha's activities?
2. Is Martha licensed to load Netscape 3.0? Is this use permitted and authorized by either the school administration or the manufacturer?
3. Is Martha authorized to set up e-mail accounts or to provide training for her faculty?
4. Is Martha really helping to ease the load for Betsy, or is she circumventing the established procedure?

10.3. Enough Time or Not Enough Time?

Each spring, Marta Luna takes a practicum student from the Smith University Library School. Marta has supervised about ten future library media specialists over the years and is proud of the role she has played in their professional development. This year Marta has agreed to take two students in a very unusual format.

The State Department of Education, which certifies school library media specialists, requires that each individual complete 300 hours of supervised practice. Since the state certification covers grades K through 12, the requirement is that the hours be split—150 in an elementary or K–6 environment and the remaining 150 in a secondary or 7–12 environment.

This year the schools in Central City are desperate for school library media specialists. There are seven schools without certified personnel and the Human Resources Department has publicized widely for additional staff. Two people who apply are not certified but are certainly eligible for an emergency or short-term certificate. They both have an MLS and several years of experience—one in academic libraries and the other in public libraries. Both have about four years of experience, but neither has ever taught. Since the final decision about hiring in Central City is up to the individual schools, both of these gentlemen are hired by two very desperate schools who use a one-time waiver of certification. Both men are told that they have one calendar year in which to complete twelve credits—six in practicum and six in literature of children and young adults. Neither expects any difficulty completing the work in children's and young adult literature but both are unsure of how to do a practicum, given their full-time work status.

Enter Marta Luna. Marta opens the doors of her school's library media center before each school day begins and keeps them open after school each day. She does two extra hours, without pay, as a service to her school. During these two hours Marta circulates books, does some reference work, and does most of her shelving. The before school program is quite busy, but since 80 percent of her school's students are brought in by bus only a few students from the neighborhood can take advantage of the after school hours. Marta offers to supervise both Barry and Bob, the two new hires with waivers. She talks with Dr. Cherwinski, the coordinator at the university, who goes along with the plan. Barry and Bob will each work ten hours per week at Marta's library media center. They will learn how to operate the on-line catalog, become familiar with the various CD products, process and catalog new materials, and assist with answering reference questions. Because of the hours involved, their contact with middle school children will be minimal. They will not plan lessons cooperatively with teachers, nor will they teach lessons.

Working ten hours per week, in just fifteen weeks each man will complete the required 150 hours in a secondary environment. The remaining 150 hours will be performed while they are on the job in their respective elementary schools. Here, they will continue to work as a fully certified school library media specialist and Marta will approve their lesson plans and twice spend an entire day at their schools. Working six hours per day, in just twenty-five days both men will complete their elementary practicum.

Marta is extremely happy with the arrangement. She will get two valuable extra pairs of hands during the morning rush and will get some help at the end of the day to clean up, back up, and so on. She doesn't think about the fact that neither Barry nor Bob will have any classroom management experience at the middle or secondary level, nor will they have the opportunity to present a lesson or to collaborate with teachers. She doesn't realize that she is getting professional library-trained clerical assistants. Dr. Cherwinski has tremendous faith in Marta and her program. Over the years nearly twelve practicum students have begun their professional careers under her direction. Each and every one of them raved about Marta and went on to successful employment.

Questions

1. Why does the district and the state allow this type of practicum?
2. Who is responsible for stopping this? Should it be stopped?
3. Why is it important for future library media specialists to learn about managing classes or collaborating with teachers?
4. Will Bob and Barry be able to do their future jobs, even with this limited type of practicum?
5. Is their practicum at the elementary school, where they are working, getting paid, and getting practicum credit, a better experience?
6. How will Marta approach supervising them at their own schools?

10.4. Do We Need a Library Media Center in the School?

Carpenter Street Middle School has been closed for ten years. The city used the building for a few of these years as a warehouse, but lately it has just been boarded up. The brick and stone edifice casts a long shadow on the surrounding land. Recently, the neighborhood around Carpenter Street has been the site of many new building programs. There are two units of cluster housing and a condo unit that holds forty families. In addition, the demographics of the surrounding neighborhoods have caused the city to consider reopening Carpenter Street Middle School.

Because the reopening of Carpenter Street Middle School will involve the busing of many students and the redistribution of students in grade 6 at several of the large elementary schools, the city is holding public hearings on the prospect. Parents of any children who might be affected by the reopening have been sent notices about the date, time, and place of the hearings. The building supervisor for the district as well as the superintendent and several program supervisors will be at the hearings. They will present a floor plan of Carpenter Street Middle School and also an introduction to the programs that will be offered there. It is hoped that a wide variety of social services will be offered to the students who attend Carpenter along with both before and after school programs. The district also hopes to secure funding to offer a program for teachers to act as mentors to other teachers. In this capacity, teachers will be asked to apply for positions at Carpenter and will be expected to hold dual certifications, have at least seven years of teaching experience, hold a graduate degree, and the like.

Sokha Chu is the library media specialist at another middle school in the district. He hears about the reopening of Carpenter Street School and wants to find out about plans for the school. He goes to one of the open meetings. There, he discovers that there is no plan to put a library media center in the newly reopened, renovated school. Sokha is dumbfounded. At the conclusion of the meeting he speaks with the superintendent and the library media supervisor. Both assure him that the information needs of the children at Carpenter Street will be met by the public library.

The public library has a branch next door to the Carpenter Street Middle School. The branch is large, but the staff is a small one. The branch is currently open two days a week from 12 P.M. to 5 P.M. and the other three days from 9 A.M. to 5 P.M. It is not open on weekends. Sokha is not familiar with this particular branch but does tell the superintendent and district library media supervisor that he cannot imagine a public library branch taking the place of a school's library media center.

The next day, after school, Sokha visits the branch of the public library next door to Carpenter Street Middle School. He notes that they have a small picture book collection but almost no young adult titles. The reference collection consists of a few encyclopedias (at least four years old) and a few almanacs and atlases. There are insufficient numbers to support any type of classroom assignments. There are no CD-ROM products at the public library and no indexes to periodicals. The periodicals at the public library are few and mostly at a higher reading level than one would expect at a middle school. Sokha knows the librarian who works at this branch and talks with her about the plans for school use of the library.

In their conversation Sokha finds out that the librarian is really an intern at the public library and has just begun to work on her MLS. She is anxious to work with school children but is not sure how things will work out. Will she go to their school with books on a cart or will they come to her? She is not certified and so cannot be with the children without a certified person in the room. Sokha is not at all encouraged by the focus the district's school library media services will take if the schools adopt the model of having the public library provide school services.

Sokha knows people on the school board, at the local university, and in the community. He doesn't know what to do, but he doesn't favor allowing Carpenter Street Middle School to open without a media center staffed by a fully certified school library media specialist.

Questions

1. Should Sokha become involved with this situation, or should he urge the district library media supervisor to take the lead?
2. What role should Sokha take? Activist? Supportive?
3. Can the public library, if the resources were increased, take the place of the school's library media center?
4. Can the public library branch fulfill its public mission as well as that of a school library media center?
5. Is the cost of installing a library media center a legitimate factor here?

III

HIGH SCHOOL OR SECONDARY SCHOOL LIBRARY MEDIA CENTERS

11
Leadership, Planning, and Management

11.1. New Services

Kris Depow was faced with a dilemma, one that she wasn't sure was good or bad. She paced up and down in the library, absent-mindedly shelving books and rearranging materials, all the while pondering what to do next. Her problem was one of almost too much of a good thing. A too-successful promotional project had threatened to overwhelm the library media center and she needed to bring it under control.

Kris, the local high school's media specialist, remembered back to the day when she first started her project. She had planned and planned, and the media center had just been budgeted for some new on-line services. The services would provide access to resources that could enhance teaching of the curriculum and research on projects. Kris had been eager to have them used by students and staff and devised methods for encouraging library use. She sent out notices to the teachers outlining the services and suggesting ways in which the teachers and students could use them. She put notices in the school newspaper and displays on the bulletin boards outside the library and the study halls. She also enlisted the help of the principal, who permitted her to make entertaining promotional announcements with voice and sound effects on the public-address system. In addition, she told the principal that she could help him by providing him with literature searches for speeches and quick answers on statistics.

The problem was that the school population had responded to the promotional campaign in overwhelming numbers. Students and teachers filled the media center from early classes until the end of the day, anxious to use the new tools. However, not only did the students have to stand in line to use the systems on the library's single computer, but the budget for the phone service was quickly depleted and her supply of ink-jet cartridges and printer paper disappeared. Kris was now faced with students who felt disappointed and teachers who wanted special services. Even the principal had created a problem by requesting numerous searches and had offered Kris's service in finding resources for board of education members and their families.

The situation was out of hand, and Kris was concerned that she might need to discontinue the services. She felt that she had done the right thing in providing expanded resources for her school, but perhaps there should be another way to handle access to the sources.

Questions

1. Is charging for printing or the paper a good solution?
2. Do the library's users need to print information, or can they just take notes?
3. Is having only one computer adequate?
4. Did Kris do enough planning before she launched into the project?
5. How should she have planned?

11.2. Crumbs and Cockroaches

Memorial High School, located in the urban city of Titusville, had always been the site of an active community group. Parent associations held book sales there, the local clerical group maintained an after school program in the auditorium, some of the mayor's subcommittees conducted hearings and workshops there, and the school board held its meetings in the building. It was the latter use that was of concern to Daisy Freeman, the library media specialist, for she had recently uncovered a problem.

The school board met monthly in the Memorial media center, and Daisy had never been comfortable with that arrangement. The problem wasn't that the members rearranged the chairs and tables; she was always able to right the room early the next morning before the students arrived. It wasn't even the crumpled paper that she often found strewn around the room; that could also be picked up. It was the marks and stains she found on the tables from the cups of water and coffee consumed by the board members. One time she had even found a coffee stain on the floor; fortunately the custodian had been able to remove it.

Daisy had spoken to the principal about the marks, but he had told her that there was nothing that could be done. "The board members are important people, and they have a right to conduct their meeting any way they wished," he said. Daisy had believed this and had suffered in silence, covering over the marks as best she could.

And now this latest situation had arisen. One of the students had come to her and reported that she had seen bugs crawling around the books. Daisy went to investigate and had seen several cockroaches sitting on top of some volumes in the stacks. She remembered that at the last board meeting the refreshments included cookies and there were crumbs on the floor the following morning. Apparently the insects had had a field day with the crumbs and had made the media center their home. Daisy went to see the custodian who promised to come and spray as soon as possible. Daisy then went to the principal's office and told him of the infestation. She was particularly concerned about what would happen to the books and told the principal that she would contact the union and the Parent/Teacher's Organization if he would not do something about the situation.

The principal was very annoyed at Daisy's attitude and told her that her veiled threat was inappropriate. He suggested, instead, that Daisy should make arrangements to have the custodian clean after every meeting, and if the custodian could not do it Daisy should clean the center herself. He felt that service to the board of education was very important and that staff should do all they could to help.

Daisy left the principal's office in a very disturbed frame of mind. She read over the union contract's description of duties and time of service and found that the principal's suggestions were contrary to the terms of the agreement. She debated about what to do next, since service was at the core of the school's philosophy and Daisy also believed in providing for the needs of all school-related activities.

Questions

1. What should Daisy do next?
2. Did Daisy do the right thing by threatening to contact the union?

3. Should Daisy have done more right from the beginning when she first noticed problems?
4. Should Daisy have established a policy about food in the library that would have covered both school and after school hours?

11.3. Budgets: Coping with a Changing School Population

Octavio Adoni was almost at his wit's end. The principal in his school had just informed him that the budget for the library media center for next year was due in two weeks and that Octavio needed to include provisions for the new students that were expected to attend the school the coming year. He also mentioned that the budget should include all facets of the library, from personnel to materials.

As a media specialist new to both the profession and this midsized high school, Octavio felt panic when he heard the principal's words. Nothing in his studies had prepared him for this approach; the only mention of budgeting had been a straight provision for materials. His field experience had been in a very different media center and the budget there had been a little broader in scope. This present situation was quite a contrast, for the school was undergoing an increase in the number of students expected to enroll, along with a change in the ethnic and economic background in the incoming students.

Once the initial shock of the notice wore off, Octavio tried to analyze the problem. There were so many things to think about: new materials in different languages and formats; perhaps a clerk to help with the daily running of the media center and translation of titles; automation for the circulation system and an on-line catalog; and some new furniture for the reading area and shelving for special language materials. These were just a few of the items that popped into Octavio's head. He wrote down these variable and fixed factors and then set about organizing them into discrete areas. He assigned a label to each of the facets he identified and then arranged the categories into groups. He ended up with sections called materials, facilities, and personnel. Then he realized that he had no idea of how much money he was supposed to include in the budget request.

Octavio approached the principal and inquired about the sum of money involved and the depth of detail needed for the budget. The principal replied with the amount that had been allotted to the media center. He also mentioned that specific names of items, along with their corresponding costs, were required. He informed Octavio that the information should be typed on order forms, along with an outline of how the pieces fit into a budget outline. He advised Octavio to consult the school's business manager to find out the names of the dealers that were acceptable for purchasing purposes.

In regard to personnel, the principal informed Octavio that a memorandum of need should be composed and should include such items as number of hours, pay per hour, and the duties that were to be assumed. He then told Octavio to get busy on his assignment, because time was limited.

Octavio wasn't sure where to turn first, but he knew he needed help.

Questions

1. Should Octavio use the *Information Power* guidelines to help him justify his budget requests?
2. It is obvious that Octavio had had little warning that the budget process was imminent. What should he have done before this time?
3. What elements of the budget should have been included in Octavio's proposal to cover this situation?
4. With whom should Octavio consult at this point?

11.4. The Hours in the Day: Flexible Scheduling

Iris Barden walked quickly into the teachers' room. Her face was flushed with excitement and she sat down next to two of the teachers who were just finishing their lunch. Iris had spent the morning talking with the media specialists in the elementary schools in East Milford, and she had come away with an idea that she wanted to share with her colleagues at the high school.

The concept that thrilled Iris was that of flexible scheduling. She had read about it in educational media newsletters and had seen it mentioned as important in the *Information Power* guidelines, but had always considered it just an intellectual idea, rather than a realistic option. The media specialists at her morning meeting had recently joined together and had just received approval from the school board for implementation of the concept. They described to Iris how the schedule would work and emphasized the freedom it would give the specialists for planning and providing individualized attention to teachers and students.

The high school in East Milford was located in a medium-sized suburban community. The school served some 800 students and was staffed with approximately fifty faculty and administrators. The scheduling pattern was rather rigid, with library lessons or research time for students provided once a week. Teachers did not attend the classes in the library, so there was little interaction between research skills and instructional skills. The "special teachers" (including Iris) served as covering teachers for planning periods.

Most of the staff consider this schedule to be satisfactory, but Iris found it very confining. It gave her very little time to do anything beyond teaching, disciplining, and basic media center maintenance. She really wanted to be able to integrate the use of library resources into the needs of the curriculum.

To Iris's surprise, her two colleagues greeted her enthusiastic description with total silence, followed by cries of protest. They voiced their displeasure with flexibility, stating that it would cause chaos, and they were also distressed at the thought of losing their planning time coverage. Iris mentioned that the new schedule would enable her to spend more time working with students on specific projects and with the teachers on planning lessons and selecting resources, but that idea fell on deaf ears.

Iris was discouraged but was determined not to give up easily. She sought out two other teachers who were friends and frequent media center users. They thought the idea was an excellent one and encouraged Iris to work to make it a reality at East Milford High. They were particularly pleased with the idea of freedom for students to use the library when they needed to work on a project, either during study periods or occasionally during class time.

Questions

1. Should Iris follow up on her idea?
2. If so, how should she proceed?
3. Should she involve the administration, and when should that happen?
4. Should flexible scheduling be a contractual matter?
5. Are there any other benefits of flexible scheduling other than those mentioned by Iris and the elementary media specialists?

12
Personnel

12.1. Parent Aide Responsibilities: How Far to Go?

It was one of those days. Thomas Carter, library media specialist at Joseph Patel High School, had fixed the copy machine four times, taught five classes of library instruction with the social studies teacher, answered many students' questions, and now was faced with a complaint from another teacher who had sent a student to the media center last week to do some independent research.

Once Thomas was able to calm the teacher, he inquired about what had happened. Judy Rodriguez told Thomas that her student had approached Eli Jordan, one of Thomas's volunteer parent aides, with a question. The query was of a rather technical nature, and the student asked Eli if he could answer the question. Eli replied in the affirmative and proceeded to look through a few books on the shelf. He found a few paragraphs in one work that appeared to be relevant to the problem. He showed the sections to the student who copied them on the copier and the student then went back to the classroom.

When Judy read the student's paper she noticed a quote that did not seem to be relevant to the theme of the research. The student had cited the source, and Judy went to the media center to check on the reference. After verifying that the source and the quotation were both incorrect and inappropriate for the paper, she was very displeased and stopped Thomas to voice a complaint. She felt that Eli was out of place when he presumed to answer a question and demanded that Thomas dismiss Eli immediately.

Thomas was surprised to hear of what had happened, because he had been very pleased with the help Eli was giving to the media center. Eli was punctual and a careful worker who related well to the students and had never caused a problem before. Thomas promised Judy that he would look into the matter and take appropriate action. Judy left somewhat mollified, but Thomas knew that something needed to be done. He made himself a note to talk to Eli the next time the volunteer came in and then sat down to think seriously about how to handle the situation.

Questions

1. Should Thomas have told Eli that he should not answer questions? Should he tell volunteers to ask students to come back if the media specialist is busy?
2. Should Thomas have a volunteers' guide? What should be included in it?
3. How and what type of training should Thomas give to the media center volunteers?
4. Does this mistake warrant dismissal?

12.2. Student Volunteers: Scheduling, Duties, and Fun

Two students approached Gregory Diaz and stated that they wanted to volunteer to work in his media center. Greg questioned them about their interest in the media center and asked them what hours would be appropriate. They replied that they thought it might be fun to put the books away and to help with charging books in and out. The girls also said that they were friends and wanted to get out of study hall and work together. Greg sighed when he heard this and saw the hour of the study period. That was the same time that three other students were already working in the media center, and they were all that he could accommodate at one time. He also had a feeling that the girls were quite close and that they might spend more time talking than working.

"This is the way it always seems to happen," thought Greg, "Murphy's law in effect once again." He was reluctant to turn the girls away because he really needed help in the center. It was heavily used and shelving was always a problem, as was circulation when Greg was involved in library instruction. He suggested that they might have some other time available in their schedule and mentioned that their help would be greatly appreciated if they could find a mutually acceptable hour.

One of the girls looked at her schedule and found another free time slot. Greg checked his volunteers' schedule and stated that that time would be both acceptable and useful. The other girl was annoyed at the thought of even looking for a change and charged out of the media center. The first girl hesitated and then told Greg that she would give it a try. Greg thanked her and they set a time for orientation.

A few days later Rosie, his new student helper, came into the media center. Greg went through the usual introduction to student help routines and Rosie quickly became very proficient in shelving and backup circulation. She was arranging books in the 300 section when her girlfriend came into the media center. She walked up to Rosie and proceeded to make some comments about being special and no longer her friend. Greg walked over to the area just in time to prevent an altercation between the two girls. He asked Rosie's friend to leave and proceeded to praise Rosie for her work and help. Rosie was pleased, but Greg wondered if there would be more trouble. He did not want to hurt Rosie or have the incident have any effects upon the other student volunteers.

It was an unpleasant dilemma. Greg had always been pleased with his student helpers and had developed a rather elaborate program that included training, work, and celebration at the end of the term. The students had spent many hours working in the media center and had been an invaluable resource for Greg. It would be a shame to have that situation come to an end.

Questions

1. Was Greg right in trying to work out a different schedule rather than using both girls at the original time?
2. How should a library media specialist approach scheduling high school students for the media center?
3. How should student workers be trained? What topics should be included in the training?

12.3. Resources, Media Specialists, and Teachers: A Perfect Match, or Is It?

Marcy Hirschberg, the library specialist, hummed a little tune as she walked down the hall to the library media center. She was pleased with herself: She had finally won the first fight of what she considered to be a long hard battle. She didn't mind when one of the students in this large, overcrowded urban high school bumped into her and practically knocked her down. In the past she would have demanded an apology or detention from the student for such rudeness, but today she just smiled and continued on her way.

When she finally reached her destination, she walked up to the assistant in the media center and announced that the first breakthrough had come. She had finally established a link with the science department and had been invited to work on the curriculum revision the science teachers had proposed for next month. Marcy and Jean, the assistant, agreed to lunch together the next Saturday to spend time planning the best course of action for the media center's role in building the science curriculum.

It had taken Marcy three years to reach this point, and she was determined to make the best of it. Before, whenever she, as the new member of the school instructional team, offered to help the teachers find resources to enhance their instruction, the suggestion had fallen on deaf ears. The mention of a role in curriculum development had been met with derision and remarks that the course of instruction did not need altering. Now, things had changed. The district school board had mandated revision of curriculums and the departments were forced to reconsider their courses of study.

Marcy knew that several of the departments had already begun their revision process and that they had turned down her offers of help. The faculty were basically long-tenured teachers who were resistant to change. They were friendly but considered their classrooms their own castles and didn't encourage students to use the media center. It was a conversation that Marcy had had with Joe Swanson, the chemistry/biology teacher, that had finally turned the tide. Marcy had told Joe of a new development in biology she had read about in the paper and mentioned that she had seen a notice about an interactive program that made the biological news exciting and understandable to teachers and students. Joe was intrigued, and the discussion led to the offer of involvement in the curriculum revision.

When Jean and Marcy met, they decided to wow the science department with examples of all sorts of resources that could make learning science stimulating for students. The big day came, and Marcy went to the first meeting of the group armed with suggestions. She was pleased to see that Joe had talked with the other teachers and that they were receptive to her recommendations. They enthusiastically involved her in all the discussions and were pleased to learn of all the existing resources in the media center. A team spirit developed, and together Marcy and the science faculty planned a completely revised and updated curriculum.

Word soon spread through the school and Marcy was in demand to help other departments with their labors. Now, she was almost overwhelmed with work. She went to talk to the principal about the problem, but he just thanked her for her efforts and urged her to keep up the good work.

Questions

1. Did she and Jean use the best approach once Marcy received the offer to participate in revising the science curriculum?
2. Was Marcy correct in thinking that the media center should be involved in the curriculum revision process?
3. Should Marcy have done more than just offer to help the teachers? Would she have been correct in offering to help the students also?

12.4. Favoritism and the District Supervisor

Things were not quite right in the Orangeville school district. Jody Segear, the district media supervisor for this large rural district, had her hands full. Jay Hopkinson, the high school library media specialist, had just stormed out of her office after accusing her of favoritism and unfair treatment.

Jody sat in her chair reviewing the last few years, years marked by a developing program of service to the three elementary, two middle, and one high school that comprised the district. She had been pleased when she had been appointed to her post as district supervisor after serving as one of the elementary media specialists for four years. Jody had organized a team of the librarians and together they had planned curriculum guidelines and districtwide cooperative selection policies. They had, under her leadership, arranged for the provision of facilities for long-distance telecommunications learning in each of the schools and had developed a network of CD-ROM reference tools. They had also worked together on writing grants for materials and had implemented the resources they had been awarded.

Jody was proud of her efforts and was proud of the district and its media specialists. She pulled out the file that listed the various purchases by the schools and scrutinized them. Jay had accused her of permitting the elementary and middle school media specialists to order more materials than she allocated to him at the high school. He said that he had compared the dollar amounts for titles budgeted and that the high school suffered because high school materials were generally more expensive. He intimated that she was prejudiced toward the elementary schools, since she had come from one of them. He also mentioned that she was prejudiced against him since he was the only male media specialist.

Jody denied the charges and promised Jay that she would review his accusations and do something about them. When she asked him the cause of his discontent, Jay admitted that he had cooperated with her efforts to organize the district but that he felt that the position of district supervisor should really be his since he was a high school employee and was more able to determine the overall needs of the district. Jody was particularly upset at that comment and decided to speak to the district superintendent.

Questions

1. Does it appear that Jay was correct in his assumption about the hierarchy of control in the district?
2. Was Jay correct in his evaluation of the budget allocations?
3. Is there a formula that can equate children's, young adult, and high school literature purchases?
4. What details should Jody mention to the district superintendent?
5. Is this an issue the district superintendent should handle? Why or why not?

13
Resources and Equipment

13.1. Books, Materials, and Such: Budgeting Print and Nonprint Resources

It was such a nice, sunny, spring day and Monica White longed to go for a walk. The students in the media center had been restless all day as they also reacted to the first day of good weather in two weeks. When the last bell of the day had rung, they had abandoned the school almost in an instant, leaving the teachers in peace to work on their lesson plans and other after school activities.

Monica sighed and told herself to settle down to work. She knew that it was not only the nice weather that had affected her—she knew that she needed to make some big decisions regarding the budget, and she was reluctant to make those commitments. The principal of the school had directed her to divide her materials budget into print and nonprint resources, and Monica wasn't sure how to do this.

During the year Monica had gathered titles and reviews of works she thought might be worth ordering for the collection at budget time. She had made a point of including book and non-book titles in her selection, and had made a listing of CD-ROM and interactive media works that would enhance the curriculum.

Now the time had come to make the actual selections. Monica sorted the titles into subject areas and made a listing of the costs of the resources, also by subject. The lists and piles of titles seemed expensive and large, in fact, much over the limit of her budget. Monica wondered what to do next and thought of contacting the heads of departments and asking them for their advice in their subject areas. She realized that that wasn't practical, however, since the budget was due Monday and today was already Wednesday. Consulting with the faculty would involve careful negotiations, and there wasn't time for that.

Monica next considered the option of evaluating her present collection and making ordering decisions based upon needs in certain subject areas. She quickly dismissed that thought, since an evaluation of the collection would also be time-consuming. She also discarded the idea of looking through some articles in the library literature and picking from the titles suggested there since that would also require time to do and those titles might not be completely appropriate for her school.

Monica then jotted down some percentages that might be used as ratios for print versus nonprint orders. She toyed with 60 and 40 percent, then 50 and 50 percent, then 75 and 25 percent. She argued with herself on the merits of the print and media resources, trying to factor in the abilities of the students in the school, her desire to make the media center attractive, and the need to make wise choices for long-term use of resources.

Finally, she decided to just shuffle the piles, pick a few titles from each, and then add up the total expenditures. This would be put into budget format and print and nonprint would be determined by chance.

Questions

1. Did Monica make the correct decision on how to construct the budget?
2. Would the options that Monica considered have been effective if she had allowed enough time to use them?
3. Can you think of other options that could be used?
4. Would it have been better if Monica had planned for the budget in a systematic way during the entire school year?
5. Is there a standard way to balance print and nonprint purchases?

13.2. Equipment versus Resources: How to Go Forward?

News of the grant had been in all the papers. It had even made the local evening newscast! The superintendent of schools had been interviewed and had indicated how pleased he was that the plight of the city schools had finally been recognized. He had also informed the news reporter that he intended to place Kauku Thiuri, the high school library media specialist, in charge of expending the money from the grant.

Kauku opened the envelope from the superintendent's office and began to read the official letter of appointment. Dr. Abull, the superintendent, had noted the need to purchase materials and equipment for all the media centers in Newport. He stated that he believed that Kauku would be qualified to organize the move to raise the schools to state standards. The attachments to the letter included the terms of the grant, which had been awarded by a national organization, and the forms that were to be filled out as the grant money was used.

As soon as he finished reading the letter, Kauku headed for the principal's office. Principal Kay Bolton recognized the signs of agitation as Kauku twittled his thumbs and started his sentence several times. On the third try Kauku was finally able to blurt out his concerns as Mrs. Bolton read Dr. Abull's letter. The importance of the appointment and the magnitude of the grant were clear, and Kay told Kauku that she had every confidence in him and that she would support him in any way she could. Kauku was relieved by her words and together they began to work on an outline of what was needed to complete the charge.

Having a rough design on paper, Kauku walked back to his library media center. He began to draw a chart listing the various schools in the district and placing categories of resources, equipment, school personnel, and population in each school. He planned to contact the library media specialists in the schools to obtain the information for his chart; he realized that an inventory of available resources should be his first step.

Then Kauku looked carefully at the terms of the grant. The amount of funding was specified, but the only stipulations were that the money was to be used for electronic equipment and resources. Kauku was a bit shocked at this, because the schools in Newport were virtually computer-free. As he thought about it, Kauku realized that this was a golden opportunity to build a system for the district, but it would need to be carefully planned.

Obviously, Kauku would need to contact vendors and salespersons who were knowledgeable about school situations and computer applications. The key point that came to his mind was the question of the relationship of equipment to software resources. Which system or systems should be purchased? Which programs would be needed? Or should the programs be considered first and the equipment next? What were the possibilities of networking within library media centers and across schools? What about including administrative programs?

This all appeared to be a tall order, and Kauku decided that another chart was appropriate. Instead of listing inventory, this one would list the pros and cons of various approaches and would leave spaces to include notes and to insert money totals for the different categories included.

Once the information on the charts had been analyzed, Kauku would consult the appropriate school personnel and then make recommendations for purchases. This seemed to be a feasible way to approach the expenditure of the grant funds and Kauku decided to spend the next week, spring vacation week, finding out as much information as he could.

Questions

1. Is Kauku's plan workable?
2. Did he leave out any elements of planning?
3. Which does come first—the equipment or the software?
4. Will it be feasible to do this type of research during vacation week? How will this affect his timetable?

13.3. Cooperative Purchasing—or We Shall Lose!

"Cooperative purchasing": somehow the term had never crossed Sesay Amoebong's mind before. That is, until today when Joan Eisenberg, one of the library media specialists, mentioned it at the district high school library media specialists meeting. She had talked about it as the library media specialists compared their budgets and had come to the conclusion that times were getting tougher and tougher and funding was tight.

It had been just a quick remark, but Sesay seized upon the concept as he drove back to Lincoln High and returned to his media center. He looked around the room and in his mind reviewed the questions he had fielded just that day as students approached him seeking sources to answer their assignments. Several of the queries could have been more fully answered if the appropriate resources had been on the shelves of the library media center. Sesay had been somewhat alarmed as he sensed the inadequacies of his collection and had resolved to try to do something about it.

A survey of options had crossed Sesay's mind: demanding a bigger share of the school budget, approaching the school's PTO, or seeking a grant for additional funding. Each of these were possibilities, but each would require a great deal of planning and public relations. These solutions also might only provide short-term relief. Sesay had not been sure that he had the time or ability to pursue any or all of these methods.

Cooperative purchasing, however, seemed to be a feasible alternative. If all the high school library media specialists worked together, they could survey their respective holdings and then choose one subject area for which each school would develop an in-depth collection. The group had already agreed that they would stress with students and teachers that assignments needed to be planned out so that sufficient lead time would be allotted to allow for research activities.

In addition, they had stressed in their bibliographic instruction sessions that one subject needed to be searched for in several resources. Information also could be obtained from another school. The district already had an interlibrary loan route, and the exhange of resources and printouts could be facilitated by that daily delivery. In fact, perhaps the public library could become part of that loop of information exchange.

Cooperative weeding might also fit into the concept of resource sharing, since subject-specific materials could be shifted from building to building. Even older editions of some works could be kept by the library media centers with certain in-depth collections and used for historical perspectives. Having schools specialize in certain subject areas would save money. Of course, basic tools would be purchased for every school, but concentrating the collections would spread out budget allocations.

Sesay was excited about these ideas and resolved to try to call the group together as soon as possible. He would approach the members with his plans and try to gain their support. Then they could each approach their individual school administrators with the ideas and collectively address the school board with a plan of action.

Questions

1. Can Sesay gain support from his colleagues to propose cooperative selection and weeding?

2. While Sesay thought of the interlibrary loan delivery system as a means of obtaining materials, he did not consider phone contact between library media centers. Would a phone or fax line be useful for facilitating communications and expediting quick access to information?
3. Is including the public library in this plan practical?
4. How should Sesay and the other library media specialists approach their administrators and the school board? Should they reveal all of their proposals at one meeting or make suggestions gradually or by priority?

13.4. Bilingual or Multilingual Resources: Which Way to Go?

Amos Harrison High School was located in the middle of the city and was in the midst of a major change in student population. The previous students had been primarily the children of fabric weavers and light industrial employees. Now the economic nature of the city had changed, and the school had students from families who were on welfare or barely subsistence wages. The school was filled with children who spoke a variety of languages, had differing religious backgrounds and family structures, and had varying levels of reading ability.

Rolanda Davis, Amos Harrison's library media specialist, wrote to her brother of how difficult it was to provide library media resources for these diverse students. She also mentioned how tough it was to communicate with them. Her brother, Philip, was also a high school library media specialist, but he worked in a smaller school where the students primarily spoke Spanish. He replied to Rolanda that he was facing the same problem, and even though he was Spanish-speaking himself, he found it difficult to provide Spanish-English resources for his students.

It was comforting to Rolanda that her problem was not unique, but it reinforced her sense of the seriousness of the situation. She appreciated the need for a solution to the problem and resolved to take some action that would benefit both her school and her brother's.

In his letter Philip had mentioned providing materials in a bilingual format. Rolanda realized that that was one approach to use for acquiring resources. As she thought about it, she also considered the idea of materials in a single foreign language that would provide comfort and continuity for the students. Or, there was always the idea of having materials only in English and forcing the students to learn that language.

Rolanda felt that the decision was a big one and that she would need the support of the principal, Mirelle Johnson. She made an appointment to see Ms. Johnson. Then she had another thought. Perhaps the format should also be taken into account. Rolanda had visited one of the elementary schools in the city and had seen a demonstration of a computerized bilingual program in one of the learning centers.

Back in her media center Rolanda ruminated on the idea of a media-driven approach to the problem. The program she had seen in the elementary school was on a very basic level and had provided the students with many bells and whistles that reinforced concepts. As she thought about it, Rolanda realized that the students in her school would probably respond to a similar approach, provided the subject matter of the story or factual information was on a high school student's emotional level. She had been taught that the vocabulary and reading level could be slightly higher or lower than the student's age level, but the affective content should remain at age level. She also remembered the precept that the subject matter should be pertinent to the students' experience.

While this last concept might be difficult to include in her selection criteria, Rolanda felt it was a necessary part of the process. She had often thumbed through computer program catalogs not looking for anything in particular, but even in that brief overview she recalled little that would relate to these students' background experiences.

By the time Rolanda had her appointment with Mirelle, she had a plan written. She explained that she would like to propose a budget for bilingual materials and equipment that would be cataloged and housed in the library media center. She would provide teachers with lists of the programs available in the hope that the teachers would either refer individual students or entire classes to the resources. As a coda to her presentation, she would search out publishers that provided diverse language materials and purchase their publications.

Mirelle thought the plans sounded feasible and promised to find funding to provide the necessary resources, both in forms of hardware and software. Rolanda was pleased and later wrote a letter to her brother about her plan.

Questions

1. Did Rolanda come up with the best solution to her problem?
2. Should Rolanda exclude print materials in different languages?
3. Is the bilingual approach the best one? Should the students be provided with materials in their own language only or in English only?
4. Is it possible to provide materials in approximately twenty different languages for the library media center?
5. Should the school have a statement of purpose that covers bilingual/mulitilingual matters? What should such a statement include?
6. Do we do students a disservice by providing an educational program in a language other than English, considering that in most areas they must enter the work force as English-speaking adults?
7. Should Rolanda search for bibliographies that have both print and nonprint materials for Spanish-speaking students?
8. Should Rolanda join curriculum committees?

14
Facilities

14.1. Whence the Computers: Library or Laboratory?

Kurt Matthew paced back and forth in the library media center. It was after school and things had quieted down enough for Kurt to think. Thinking time was essential since Kurt needed to respond to the question the principal had posed to him earlier in the day.

As he mentally reviewed the conversation with Principal Johnson, Kurt realized that the future of computerized information resources in Memorial High School depended upon how well he could formulate a plan for housing the computers that had been approved by the board of education. He knew that the science and math department heads had asked for a computer lab to be located in the far wing of the school, near their classrooms.

Kurt decided that his plan would emphasize computer access for the entire school, rather than a lab for certain areas. Placing computers in the library media center would make the new technology available for all students and staff to use during the day, and during the center's evening hours. In addition, he reasoned, he could make some basic reference resources available on CD-ROM, such as *Infotrac,* as well as curriculum programs and utilities that would apply to the entire school. It was an exciting prospect.

As he looked around his center, Kurt noticed he would have to rearrange it in order to accommodate the new computers. In fact, as he surveyed the space, he realized that there probably was not enough room to house all the equipment he had imagined.

After considering several possibilities, Kurt decided that perhaps the lab wasn't a bad idea after all, if it would be adjacent to the library media center. If the classroom next to the center could be converted into a lab space and the wall between the rooms at least partially removed, there would be a concentrated area where computers could be networked and students could receive instruction in using the machines and programs. Yes, that would be the plan: a bank of connected computers with a variety of programs and information resources sited in a laboratory that was part of the library media center.

Next he would consider the types, numbers, and cost of the computers and programs that he would like to have in this laboratory. Mr. Johnson had not mentioned a budget figure for this project. Kurt decided to use a proactive approach and write up his estimated budget for the laboratory as he envisioned it.

Questions

1. Did Kurt consider all the options available to him?
2. How will the laboratory be maintained and controlled?
3. Was Kurt correct in deciding to just present a budget, rather than asking if there were limits?
4. Should Kurt have involved other staff members in his deliberations?
5. Will there be problems with the math and science departments over control of the laboratory since they wanted the computers in their own departments? Would teachers be more apt to integrate the use of computers in their own subject areas if a computer were to be placed in each classroom?
6. Should Kurt take a workshop or course in the uses of computers in library media centers before giving a plan to the principal?
7. If the computers had been approved by the board of education without Kurt's knowledge, what problems would this present?
8. How will staff and students be trained to use this new equipment? Whose budget item will this be?

14.2. To Decorate or Not?

During the last week of August the teachers at Montclair High were setting up their classrooms for the new academic year. Trudy Rodriguez, the new library media specialist, was busy preparing bulletin boards, placing new books on display on top of the low shelves, and arranging pictures and items on the walls of the library media center. The theme of these displays was "literature for autumn," and they added a bright splash of color to the otherwise drab-looking room.

Rhonda Warwick and Bob Marker were walking down the hallway and happened to glance into the media center. Rhonda was aghast at what she saw: leaves, pictures of children dancing, pumpkins, and other similar artifacts of fall. Ms. Warwick was one of the most senior teachers in the building and she felt that the dignity of the school was being compromised by the display of such elementary items. Bob, on the other hand, thought that the theme and touch of color were very appropriate and gave life to the media center. He had been at Montclair for almost as many years as Rhonda and had always felt that the school was a rather somber, forbidding place. He silently applauded Trudy even as Rhonda berated her and threatened to mention this new approach to the principal.

Trudy was upset, because she believed the color and display would attract students to the library media center. Her basic philosophy was that enhancing the print-rich environment would have a positive impact on the perception and use of the center's resources for students of any grade level. She certainly did not want to alienate any of the staff members nor did she want to lose her new job. She assured Rhonda and Bob that she would change her approach and place more traditionally high school decorations in a few places.

Questions

1. Did Trudy make the correct decision? Should she have followed her initial instincts and left the items in place?
2. Should high school library media centers be decorated? If so, in what fashion?
3. Should schools have an overall policy on decorating?

4. What right did Rhonda have to assume she could criticize another colleague's decoration?
5. Should Trudy go to the principal and ask to have the entire media center decorated? Does this action require preapproval?

14.3. Control of the Phone and Fax

Li Wang sighed as the phone rang again. She walked across the library media center and tried to control the tone of exasperation in her voice as she answered the fourth call that hour for a faculty member. She put the call on hold and sent one of her student assistants to inform the teacher that she was wanted on the phone. Just then the fax machine started to print out a message from another school. Li checked the address on the facsimile and noted that it was a transmission for the vice principal. Li asked another student to take the fax to the administrative office. The machine began to print out another message, and Li felt as if she would scream!

What had happened to her plans to use the phone and fax machine for library media center purposes? As the library media specialist, she had thought that phone calls would concern reference questions and other library-related matters. Instead, the two pieces of equipment had almost become albatrosses around her neck as they served as the communication hub of the school. Li had become the auxiliary phone operator for Ridge High. In addition, the cost of the paper and the phone line for the fax machine was being charged to the library media center.

Li realized that she had made a mistake in not establishing guidelines for use when she had proposed the addition of the two machines. She had assumed that the other staff members would respect her wishes for library use, but the convenience of the phone led them to use it for their purposes also. The same was true of the fax machine. It had become a real nuisance as messages about doctors' appointments and other personal subjects had become the norm.

Now was the time for action, before the situation became intolerable. Li decided to approach the principal to ask his support for guidelines, even though they were long overdue. John Ziso had been her mentor for several years and had enthusiastically endorsed her original request. He listened to her complaints and agreed that there was a problem. He said that he would be willing to listen to her guidelines after she had prepared them, but he warned that the staff would be resistant to any changes. His advice was to propose moderate standards that emphasized library use but left space for other messages and transactions.

Li left the office feeling half relieved and half anxious. Mr. Ziso had suggested an alternative, but it would be a very difficult one to establish. Li decided to try to write guidelines and to hope for the best.

Questions

1. What policies should be established regarding the use of the phone and the fax machines when they are placed in the school library media center?
2. Are there any issues other than convenience and cost to be considered in this situation?
3. Is Mr. Ziso's solution feasible?
4. Should personal messages be sent and received on a regular basis by the school's phone or fax?
5. Should the school provide phone lines and fax lines in the teachers' room? Would this relieve the media specialist from being a messenger? Would this relieve the financial strain on the media center budget? How would it affect the school budget?

14.4. The Virtual Library

Eyvlonda Gonzales sat at her desk late one Friday afternoon reviewing her budget and looking over the number of networking licenses and computer stations that she had requested for the past year. She smiled to herself as she realized that those multiple programs and equipment setups filled the last step in her plan for the school's virtual library.

A scant three years had passed since she had first proposed the concept of total school library service at a faculty meeting. She had sold the faculty and the administration on the idea of having computers in the library media center with access to the on-line catalog, *Infotrac, The Encarta*

Multimedia Encyclopedia, the Internet, and several other library reference resources. Students and teachers could search for information right in their classes and write papers and other research assignments at their desks.

This had sounded like a library media specialist's dream of a service that reached out to the entire school. It seemed like a dream during the past year when the computers were finally networked and the programs were accessible throughout the school. The teachers had praised her and were very pleased that they had instant access. A frown suddenly passed across Eyvlonda's face as she recalled a comment she had overheard from one teacher to another in the faculty room. The teacher had complained that she wasn't really comfortable with using the computers and was unsure of how to access the Internet. The teacher replied that he had begun to realize that an extra burden had been placed upon him and that he, too, was uncomfortable with teaching the information-searching techniques that had previously been taught by Eyvlonda.

As she thought some more, Eyvlonda began to have some doubts about her concept of the virtual library. Perhaps there were some issues she had not considered when she conceived this idea. She had not thought of the need for training for searching/computer skills and had not considered the control over supplies, upgrades, etc. So far she had been lucky—the computers had been trouble-free and the vendors had been anxious to keep her subscriptions up to date. But the Internet had expanded almost exponentially the past year, and Eyvlonda realized that she needed to address issues of access and control, especially as the students established Internet accounts and began to search the Net.

The more she thought, the more concerned Eyvlonda became. Was the virtual library becoming out of control? Could her collections be distributed throughout the school? Would the faculty assume her role of instructor and organizer of information? Eyvlonda realized that she needed to talk to her principal about a plan for the future.

Questions

1. What should Eyvlonda have done to plan for this schoolwide library?
2. What policies should have been formulated and written in the planning stages of this virtual library?
3. Who should provide training to teachers? To students?
4. Should there be two separate training programs—one about computer use and the other software use?

15
District, Regional, and State Leadership

15.1. Regional Networks: To Join or Not to Join?

All Joanne Practico could think of was the regional network. Four of the state counties had joined together as a library consortium and this new grouping was seeking members. The consortium was headed by the director of one of the area's large public libraries and the incorporated board was composed of eight members that represented all types of libraries within the region.

The group's bylaws called for cooperation among libraries, dispersal of state funds for services rendered, and specified three levels of service: reference, interlibrary loan, and delivery. Membership without charge was open to any library within the region, provided the library adhered to the service requirements. The larger libraries would serve as reference referral sites for the smaller libraries which had limited resources. There was also a provision for a regionwide borrower's card, but each library was free to set loaning restrictions on heavy-use items. Plans were also under way for establishing a regional on-line catalog.

Joanne, Moore High School's library media specialist, had attended the third meeting of the group, where they talked about the various services that could be cooperatively shared. She had been particularly excited about the idea of a regionwide delivery system that could provide daily drop-offs of materials. Joanne felt this was a real boon for the students in Moore High, a medium-sized facility with barely adequate resources.

An expanded interlibrary loan system was to be provided by the largest library in the region. The library was on the OCLC network and had offered to provide locational holding information to region members as their contribution to the consortium. Joanne knew this was an important service that could help her to find resources located outside of her library.

The consortium had also agreed to survey member libraries to locate special collections in each library. This information would be made available in a directory, and the specified library would provide special reference service on that topic. There had even been a discussion of providing access to the Internet for member libraries.

Joanne mentally reviewed her collection and began to wonder if she had anything to offer to the consortium. There was a small local history collection that was used by the high school seniors to prepare their final projects, but the collection at the local public library was more complete. Her circulating collection was a typical school collection and was geared primarily to the curriculum. It was not strong in any one area but was spread across the field of knowledge. Then Joanne had an inspiration. She had a good collection of teacher resource materials that she had ordered for the faculty. Perhaps that could be the collection of expertise that could be offered by Moore High School.

Joanne decided that it was now time to approach the principal to ask for his support so Moore High could join the consortium. She could emphasize the free membership, the reciprocal benefits of joining the group, and her willingness to supply reference assistance regarding teacher resources. This seemed to be a golden opportunity to obtain expanded services for the school at a relatively small price.

Questions

1. Was Joanne being too optimistic about the benefits to be gained by Moore High School?
2. Is it possible that Joanne might find the regional consortium controlling her collection and reference time?
3. Joanne's collection consists primarily of print materials. In order to benefit from some of the region's plans, Joanne's school might have to invest heavily in new technology and software. Does it appear that this is possible, based upon Joanne's present barely adequate resources?

15.2. State Conference Presenter: Is It Possible?

Marcantonio Muller was a member of his state's educational media association, and he was at the meeting when it issued a call for presentations at its spring conference. Marco, a school library media specialist, had sent in a suggestion for a workshop on searching the Internet using school facilities, and he had just received a letter informing him that his proposal had been accepted. He was thrilled!

In his initial proposal Marco had suggested that a speaker present an overview of the various searching mechanisms and then a panel discussion be held on the various highlights and problems that could be encountered as faculty and students accessed the Internet. The acceptance panel of the state conference committee had particularly liked Marco's ideas on the perils of Internet searching, considering it to be a relevant topic for the convention.

Marco rushed down to Principal Feldman's office and was fortunate to be able to gain immediate admittance. After reading the letter, Dr. Feldman congratulated Marco and then began to discuss specifics. While the school was happy to support Marco in his professional obligations, there were certain restrictions that were applied to all school staff members.

Marco had never had any time conflict between his school duties and his responsibilities to the educational media association. Membership meetings were held in the evening or on weekends, so it did not require any time away from school. The annual conference time had been taken out of Marco's professional leave allocation, so that had not been a problem.

It was certainly an honor to be included on the conference program, but glory and growth aside, what about the time spent planning the session? Would the school be required to pay for the phone calls made by Marco as he assembled his program? And what about expenses incurred at the conference? Since Marco was a presenter at the program, would the school be expected to pay for his expenses as a token of support?

Dr. Feldman stressed that funds were tight and that scheduling at the school was also difficult. If Marco decided to have a practice session before the actual presentation, would a substitute be required to fill his library media center assignment for that also? Marco did not answer Dr. Feldman's questions at that time. He wanted a chance to prepare his response and to make a few phone calls before he committed himself. Dr. Feldman granted him this request, and Marco returned to his media center.

Questions

1. Should Marco still plan to make his presentation at the conference?
2. Is Dr. Feldman being unreasonable?
3. Does the school have an obligation to support the professional growth of its staff members? Would this bring positive publicity to the school?

15.3. Districtwide Cooperation: Is There a Leader?

Two weeks had passed since the Southville School District had received word of the accreditation visit by the state department of education that was due in three months. All of the programs in the schools, as well as the staff credentials, school expenditures, and testing results were to be examined.

Dr. Taylor, superintendent of schools, had called a professional day for the entire district so that plans for the visit could be made. After a brief discussion of the purpose and content of the visit, Dr. Taylor had asked the staff to group together by discipline and grade levels. Each group was to elect a group leader who would be responsible for submitting the required paperwork, holding meetings for his/her division, and making sure that that division's report was prepared in a timely fashion.

Lynda Friedman, the high school media specialist, had been elected by her group as the natural leader. She had the largest collection, had seniority, and had experience with accreditation visits. Lynda accepted the post but with the proviso that all the media specialists in the district provide her with the necessary information for each of their media centers for a proper report. She had formed that stipulation so that all the librarians would feel that they were part of a team.

While this was a rather forced way to encourage cooperation, Lynda viewed it as a good opportunity to bring the media specialists together and to develop a districtwide plan for the future of the library media centers. The report for the evaluation included a section on plans for the future direction of the units, in terms of both philosophy and resources. Lynda was determined to use this report as a concrete plan for the future that all of the specialists could adopt as a basis for their own.

Lynda and the group had also agreed to use a timetable for the preparation of the reports. Each member had two weeks to write up an overview of the collections and services provided by his or her media center. Then they had another two weeks to write what they expected to achieve in the coming two years and then, again, in the following ten years. There had been some grumbling about the amount of work these reports would require, but all agreed that it was necessary. When Lynda suggested that they all gather together for a pizza and ice cream party when the reports were completed, there was total agreement.

Questions

1. Did Lynda approach the preparation of the report in a satisfactory manner?
2. Do you think her time line is feasible?
3. Was Lynda correct in thinking that a districtwide library media specialists team could grow out of this evaluation?

15.4. Serving on a Statewide Task Force: Is It Possible?

Hiram Bigelow was in the middle of a tug-of-war between the chairperson of a statewide library task force and the superintendent of his own school district. Hiram had been asked by the chairperson of the committee to serve as a school library media specialist on a task force that was exploring the development of statewide library services.

The problem began when the superintendent had received a copy of the letter that the committee chairperson had sent to Hiram asking for help. The superintendent grasped the importance of this appointment, but he was also aware of the large amount of time that might be required to complete such a task.

When Hiram and the principal of his high school arrived at the superintendent's office, the pros and cons of the task force service were placed on the table and each one received an in-depth analysis. The positive items included the benefits that could be derived from statewide library services and the prestige that having a member of the staff on the task force would bring to the district. This last item was good public relations for the district.

On the other hand, the negative items included the large amounts of time that might be consumed by task force work. In addition, there would be the need to provide substitute media specialists so Hiram could attend meetings or prepare reports. There might be the need to provide secretarial time for reports, and there would be additional phone and postage bills. This would need to come from district budgets, since the statewide task force was strictly voluntary, with no financial assistance provided.

At a quick glance, it appeared that the pros and cons were of almost equal weight. However, it was the administrators who were responsible for their district, and they needed to evaluate loss and benefit, both for now and in the future.

The superintendent and the principal discussed the issue a bit more and then announced that they would prefer that Hiram not accept the appointment. If he did, it would place a burden upon the district, and it would be his responsibility to assume much of the work himself. Hiram debated with himself at length and then after a long long weekend, composed a letter of regret to the chairperson of the state task force.

Questions

1. Did Hiram make the correct decision? Why or why not?
2. Were the school district administrators' concerns valid?
3. Should Hiram have at least offered to suggest another media specialist to the task force chairperson?

Appendix A

AASL Position Statement on Access to Resources and Services in the School Library Media Program: An Interpretation of the *Library Bill of Rights*

The school library media program plays a unique role in promoting intellectual freedom. It serves as a point of voluntary access to information and ideas and as a learning laboratory for students as they acquire critical thinking and problem-solving skills needed in a pluralistic society. Although the educational level and program of the school necessarily shape the resources and services of a school library media program, the principles of the *Library Bill of Rights* apply equally to all libraries, including school library media programs.

School library media professionals assume a leadership role in promoting the principles of intellectual freedom within the school by providing resources and services that create and sustain an atmosphere of free inquiry. School library media professionals work closely with teachers to integrate instructional activities in classroom units designed to equip students to locate, evaluate, and use a broad range of ideas effectively. Through resources, programming, and educational processes, students

This appendix is reprinted from the American Association of School Librarians Electronic Library published in Chicago in 1995 by the American Library Association.

and teachers experience the free and robust debate characteristic of a democratic society.

School library media professionals cooperate with other individuals in building collections of resources appropriate to the developmental and maturity levels of students. These collections provide resources which support curriculum and are consistent with the philosophy, goals, and objectives of the school district. Resources in school library media collections represent diverse points of view and current as well as historical issues.

While English is by history and tradition the customary language of the United States, the languages in use in any given community may vary. Schools serving communities in which other languages are used make efforts to accommodate the needs of students for whom English is a second language. To support these efforts, and to ensure equal access to resources and services, the school library media program provides resources which reflect the linguistic pluralism of the community.

Members of the school community involved in the collection development process employ educational criteria to select resources unfettered by their personal, political, social, or religious views. Students and educators served by the school library media program have access to resources and services free of constraints resulting from personal, partisan, or doctrinal disapproval. School library media professionals resist efforts by individuals to define what is appropriate for all students or teachers to read, view, or hear.

Major barriers between students and resources include: imposing age or grade level restrictions on the use of resources, limiting the use of interlibrary loan and access to electronic information, charging fees for information in specific formats, requiring permission from parents or teachers, establishing restricted shelves or closed collections, and labeling. Policies, procedures, and rules related to the use of resources and services support free and open access to information.

The school board adopts policies that guarantee students access to a broad range of ideas. These include policies on collection development and procedures for the review of resources about which concerns have been raised. Such policies, developed by the persons in the school community, provide for a timely and fair hearing and assure that procedures are applied equitably to all expressions of concern. School library media professionals implement district policies and procedures in the school.

—Adopted July 2, 1986; amended January 10, 1990, by the ALA Council.

Appendix B
AASL Position Paper on Information Literacy

To be prepared for a future characterized by change, students must learn to think rationally and creatively, solve problems, manage and retrieve information, and communicate effectively. By mastering information problem-solving skills students will be ready for an information-based society and a technological workplace.

Information literacy is the term being applied to the skills of information problem solving. The purpose of this position paper is to identify the key elements of information literacy and present a rationale for integrating information literacy into all aspects of the K–12 and post-secondary curriculum. Many aspects of both the school restructuring movement and library media programs relate directly to information literacy and its impact on student learning.

Today, many different groups are helping to define information literacy. For example, information literacy is one of five essential competencies for solid job performance according to the U.S. Department of Labor Secretary's Commission on Achieving Necessary Skills (SCANS). The SCANS report makes the case for developing high-performance skills to support an economy characterized by high skills, high wages, and full

This appendix is reprinted from the American Association of School Librarians Electronic Library published in Chicago in 1995 by the American Library Association.

employment. A high-skill work force is also called for in President Clinton's National Technology Policy for America.

Educators are recognizing the importance of information literacy. In 1991, the Association of Supervision and Curriculum Development (ASCD) adopted the following statements:

> Information literacy . . . equips individuals to take advantage of the opportunities inherent in the global information society. Information literacy should be a part of every student's educational experience. ASCD urges schools, colleges, and universities to integrate information literacy programs into learning programs for all students.

ASCD is one of sixty educational associations which have formed the National Forum on Information Literacy (NFIL).

Restructuring and Information Literacy

Research on the restructuring of schools calls for the teacher's role to change from a textbook lecturer to that of a coach. Students become active learners who create their own knowledge after interacting with information from a variety of resources. Learning which results from use of multiple resources is often referred to as resource-based learning.

Resource-based learning requires that students are effective users of information regardless of format. Print resources such as books and magazines as well as electronic resources such as computer databases and laser videodiscs will be used by students. Students will master information literacy skills when teachers and library media specialists guide them as they use information with a discipline or through an interdisciplinary project.

Another component of restructuring, performance assessment, flows from active resource-based learning. Learning is assessed by observing student demonstrations of ability, knowledge, or competencies. In a fully functioning performance assessment setting, student portfolios and other assessment techniques are used to measure outcomes or competencies.

Curriculum and Information Literacy

To become effective information users, students must have frequent opportunities to handle all kinds of information. Locating, interpreting, analyzing, synthesizing, evaluating, and communicating information should become a part of every subject across the curriculum. Resource-based learning calls for all members of the educational community to become partners in a shared goal, providing successful learning experiences for all students. Learning environments should be structured to allow students unlimited access to multiple resources in the classroom, the library media center, and beyond the school walls.

The principal, as instructional leader, fosters resource-based learning by providing adequate planning time and budget support. As instructional partners, the classroom teacher and library media specialist are actively involved in identifying the learning needs of the students, developing teaching units, and guiding their progress. The library media specialist facilitates activities which offer meaningful practice in using a variety of information resources.

In an effective information literacy curriculum, the student's experience with information moves away from learning traditional library location skills taught in isolation. Rather, the student learns information literacy skills, as defined in this paper, embedded into the core curriculum. Once acquired, a solid foundation of information literacy skills will prepare students for a lifetime of learning.

Library Media Programs

The role of the library media program is to ensure that students and staff are effective users of ideas and information. The library media program supports the curriculum by providing adequate resources, personnel, and training so that both students and teachers become independent users of information.

The library media specialist plays a critical role in a school's instructional program. To foster information literacy, the library media specialist:

- Works with the classroom teacher as a partner to plan, design, deliver, and evaluate instruction using a variety of resources and information problem-solving skills.
- Serves as a teacher and consultant in the transition from a textbook-centered classroom to a resource-based classroom.
- Provides leadership, expertise, and advocacy in the use of technology and resources.
- Partners with teachers to empower students to accept responsibility for their own learning, thereby becoming capable of learning over a lifetime.
- Manages a program (personnel, resources, facility, and services) in which students receive instruction and practice in the use of information. Guidance is given for reading, viewing, and listening so that students can locate resources for both personal enrichment as well as for information problem-solving.

A school library media program that is truly integrated into the school's curriculum is central to helping students master information literacy skills.

> "Ultimately, information literate people are those who have learned how to learn. They know how to learn because they know how knowledge is organized, how to find information, and how to use information in such a way that others can learn from them. They are people prepared for lifelong learning, because they can always find the information needed for any task or decision at hand."—ALA Presidential Committee on Information Literacy

Information Problem-Solving Skills

Introduction

The ability to access and use information is necessary for success in school, work, and personal life. The following steps represent the basic elements in an information literacy curriculum.

I. Defining the Need for Information

The first step in the information problem-solving process is to recognize that an information need exists and to define that need. The student will be able to:

A. Recognize different uses of information (i.e., occupational, intellectual, recreational).
B. Place the information needed within a frame of reference (who, what, when, where, how, why).
C. Relate the information needed to prior knowledge.
D. Formulate the information problem using a variety of questioning skills (i.e., yes/no, open ended).

II. Initiating the Search Strategy

Once the information problem has been formulated, the student must understand that a plan for searching has to be developed. The student will be able to:

A. Determine what information is needed, often through a series of subquestions.
B. Brainstorm ideas and recognize a variety of visual ways of organizing ideas to visualize relationships among them (i.e., webbing, outlining, listing).
C. Select and use a visual organizer appropriate to subject.
D. List key words, concepts, subject headings, descriptors.
E. Explain the importance of using more than one source of information. Identify potential sources of information.
F. Identify the criteria for evaluating possible sources (i.e., timeliness, format, appropriateness).

III. Locating the Resources

At the onset of a search a student will recognize the importance of locating information from a variety of sources and accessing specific information found within an individual resource. The student will be able to:

A. Locate print, audiovisual, and computerized resources in the school library media center using catalogs and other bibliographic tools.
B. Locate information outside of the school library media center through on-line databases, interlibrary loan, telephone, and facsimile technology.
C. Identify and use community information agencies (i.e., public and academic libraries, government offices) to locate additional resources.

D. Use people as sources of information through interviews, surveys, and letters of inquiry.
E. Consult with library media specialists and teachers to assist in identifying sources of information.
F. Access specific information within resources by using internal organizers (i.e., indexes, tables of contents, cross references) and electronic search strategies (i.e., key words, Boolean logic).

IV. Assessing and Comprehending the Information

Once potentially useful information has been located, the student uses a screening process to determine the usefulness of the information. The student will be able to:

A. Skim and scan for major ideas and key words to identify relevant information.
B. Differentiate between primary and secondary sources.
C. Determine the authoritativeness, currentness, and reliability of the information.
D. Differentiate among fact, opinion, propaganda, point of view, and bias.
E. Recognize errors in logic.
F. Recognize omissions, if any, in information.
G. Classify, group, or label the information.
H. Recognize interrelationships among concepts.
I. Differentiate between cause and effect.
J. Identify points of agreement and disagreement among sources.
K. Select information in formats most appropriate to the student's individual learning style.
L. Revise and redefine the information problem if necessary.

V. Interpreting the Information

Following an assessment of the information, the student must use the information to solve the particular information problem. The student will be able to:

A. Summarize the information in the student's own words; paraphrase or quote important facts and details when necessary for accuracy and clarity.
B. Synthesize newly gathered information with previous information.

C. Organize and analyze information in a new way.
D. Compare information gathered with the original problem and adjust strategies, locate additional information, or re-examine information when necessary.
E. Draw conclusions based on the information gathered and the student's interpretation of it.

VI. Communicating the Information

The student must be able to organize and communicate the results of the information problem-solving effort. The student will be able to:

A. Use the search information to identify the important conclusions or resolutions to the problem to be shared with others.
B. Decide on a purpose (i.e., to inform, persuade, entertain) for communicating the information and identify the intended audience.
C. Choose a format (i.e., written, oral, visual) appropriate for the audience and purpose.
D. Create an original product (i.e., speech, research paper, videotape, drama).
E. Provide appropriate documentation (i.e., bibliography) and comply with copyright law.

VII. Evaluating the Product and Process

Evaluation is the ability to determine how well the final product resolved the information problem and if the steps taken to reach the desired outcome were appropriate and efficient. Students may evaluate their own work and/or be evaluated by others (i.e., classmates, teachers, library media staff, parents). The student will be able to:

A. Determine the extent to which the conclusions and project met the defined information need and/or satisfied the assignment (i.e., how well did I do?).
B. Consider if the research question/problem, search strategy, resources, or interpretation should have been expanded, revised, or otherwise modified (i.e., what could/should I have done differently?).
C. Reassess his/her understanding of the process and identify steps which need further understanding, skill development, or practice (i.e., how can I do better in the future?).

Bibliography

American Association of School Librarians and Association for Educational Communications and Technology, *Information Power: Guidelines for School Library Media Programs* (Chicago: ALA, 1988).

American Library Association Presidential Committee on Information Literacy: Final Report (Chicago: ALA, 1989).

Eisenberg, Mike, and Bob Berkowitz. *Curriculum Initiative: An Agenda and Strategy for Library Media Programs* (Norwood, N.J.: Ablex, 1988).

Michigan State Board of Education, Position Paper on Information Processing Skills (Michigan, 1992).

"Restructuring and School Libraries—Special Issue," *NASSP Bulletin,* May 1991, pp. 1–58.

U.S. Department of Labor, The Secretary's Commission on Achieving Necessary Skills, *Learning a Living: A Blueprint for High Performance* (Washington, D.C.: U.S. Government Printing Office, 1992).

Information Literacy in Action

Students practice information literacy in many different ways. In the following scenarios that exemplify cooperative instructional efforts between teachers and library media specialists, students demonstrate their information problem-solving skills through significant learning experiences.

Scenario #1—Three students in the elementary school library media center are working at a multimedia workstation completing a report of interviews with elderly community residents. They are incorporating stories about their community during World War II, photos of some of the community residents, photos of the community from that period of time, and a table with community population figures. This report will go into each child's portfolio.

Scenario #2—In the middle school media center students are using electronic mail to work with scientists and other students on the International Arctic Project. Using the Internet, an international electronic communication network, students are sharing data from their own lake study project with students as far away as Russia. They are also following an Arctic training expedition, questioning and receiving information from the explorers.

Scenario #3—In the high school library media center students are preparing to produce a video news report set in the Civil War. They are searching the school district on-line catalog, a database of statewide library resources and on-line historical magazine indexes, and a laser disc of resources from the Library of Congress. Among the resources selected by one student are primary source newspapers, an audiotaped documentary, and an audio recording of folk songs, along with books and magazine articles. Electronic mail is used to request some items through interlibrary loan.

Scenario #4—Elementary students who are setting up a freshwater aquarium in their classroom during a study of aquatic life plan their class time with the teacher before they consult and work with the library media specialist to locate and use print and nonprint sources. They collect the materials, plants, and animals based on their completed research. The teacher and library media specialist locate biological data through the Internet and students confer with the local experts via telephone interview and Internet e-mail.

Scenario #5—A team of middle school teachers and the library media specialist plan a study of life in the Middle Ages that will involve a special mock celebration. They group students, identify projects that will be completed, and suggest roles each will play in the study. The teachers and library media specialist review the requirements and identify resources necessary, the best information access points for each group, and the most efficient scheduling of time and resource use.

Scenario #6—Advanced high school students involved in an independent study in chemistry are matched with mentors with whom they communicate through telephone and Internet. The mentors guide students in projects and suggest sources with which to work. The students negotiate with teachers on the project expectations and completion time. Information needs are formulated with the library media specialist, and materials are collected for completion of projects.

Scenario #7—A district staff development workshop is planned by a team of curriculum personnel, principals, library media specialists, and teachers. The workshop emphasis is on critical thinking skills. Information searches are completed in ERIC and other national databases to identify research in the field, people as speakers, and resources for student use. Plans are completed, packets of information collated for distribution, and the workshop sponsored.

Scenario #8—Elementary students involved in a whole language reading program listen to storytellers of folk tales before selecting related books to read. After reading, students advise the teacher and library media specialist on the themes and characters that they think they should pursue. The students, teacher, and library media specialist locate nonprint and other print sources in local and statewide catalogs for further student reading and study. Students use gathered materials for their own storytelling festival.

Developed by the Wisconsin Educational Media Association and endorsed by the Wisconsin Department of Public Instruction.

Adopted and formatted by the American Association of School Librarians, 1994. Reprinted with permission by AASL with additional scenarios by Paula Montgomery.

Adopted by the National Forum for Information Literacy, an umbrella group of over sixty organizations.

Appendix C

AASL Position Statement on Appropriate Staffing for School Library Media Centers

The success of any school library media program, no matter how well designed, depends ultimately on the quality and number of the personnel responsible for the program. A well-educated and highly motivated professional staff, adequately supported by technical and clerical staff, is critical to the endeavor.

Although staffing patterns are developed to meet local needs, certain basic staffing requirements can be identified. Staffing patterns must reflect the following principles:

1. All students, teachers, and administrators in each school building at all grade levels must have access to a library media program provided by one or more certified library media specialists working full time in the school's library media center.
2. Both professional personnel and support staff are necessary for all library media programs at all grade levels. Each school must employ at least one full-time technical assistant or clerk for each library media specialist. Some programs, facilities, and levels of service will require more than one support staff member for each professional.
3. More than one library media professional is required in many schools. The specific number of additional professional staff is determined by

This appendix is reprinted from the American Association of School Librarians Electronic Library published in Chicago in 1995 by the American Library Association.

> the school's size, number of students and of teachers, facilities, specific library program. A reasonable ratio of professional staff to teacher and student populations is required in order to provide for the levels of service and library media program development described in *Information Power: Guidelines for School Library Media Programs*.

All school systems must employ a district library media director to provide leadership and direction to the overall library media program. The district director is a member of the administrative staff and serves on committees that determine the criteria and policies for the district's curriculum and instructional programs. The director communicates the goals and needs of both the school and district library media programs to the superintendent, board of education, other district-level personnel, and the community. In this advocacy role, the district library media director advances the concept of the school library media specialist as a partner with teachers and promotes a staffing level that allows the partnership to flourish.

Appendix D
AASL Position Statement on Flexible Scheduling

Schools must adopt the educational philosophy that the library media program is fully integrated into the educational program. This integration strengthens the teaching/learning process so that students can develop the vital skills necessary to locate, analyze, evaluate, interpret, and communicate information and ideas. When the library media program is fully integrated into the instructional program of the school, students, teachers, and library media specialists become partners in learning. The library program is an extension of the classroom. Information skills are taught and learned within the context of the classroom curriculum. The wide range of resources, technologies, and services needed to meet students' learning and information needs are readily available in a cost-effective manner.

The integrated library media program philosophy requires that an open schedule must be maintained. Classes cannot be scheduled in the library media center to provide teacher release or preparation time. Students and teachers must be able to come to the center throughout the day to use information sources, to read for pleasure, and to meet and work with other students and teachers.

Planning between the library media specialist and the classroom teacher, which encourages both scheduled and informal visits, is the catalyst that makes this integrated library program work. The teacher brings to the

This appendix is reprinted from the American Association of School Librarians Electronic Library published in Chicago in 1995 by the American Library Association.

planning process a knowledge of subject content and student needs. The library media specialist contributes a broad knowledge of resources and technology, an understanding of teaching methods, and a wide range of strategies that may be employed to help students learn information skills. Cooperative planning by the teacher and library media specialist integrates information skills and materials into the classroom curriculum and results in the development of assignments that encourage open inquiry.

The responsibility for flexibly scheduled library media programs must be shared by the entire school community.

THE BOARD OF EDUCATION endorses the philosophy that the library program is an integral part of the district's educational program and ensures that flexible scheduling for library media centers is maintained in all buildings and at all levels.

THE DISTRICT ADMINISTRATION supports this philosophy and monitors staff assignments to ensure appropriate staffing levels so that all teachers, including the library media specialists, can fulfill their professional responsibilities.

THE PRINCIPAL creates the appropriate climate within the school by advocating the benefits of flexible scheduling to the faculty, by monitoring scheduling, by ensuring appropriate staffing levels, and by providing joint planning time for classroom teachers and library media specialists.

THE TEACHER uses resource-based instruction and views the library media program as an integral part of that instruction.

THE LIBRARY MEDIA SPECIALIST is knowledgeable about curriculum and classroom activities, and works cooperatively with the classroom teacher to integrate information skills into the curriculum.

Appendix E
AASL Position Statement on Preparation of School Library Media Specialists

School library media specialists have a broad undergraduate education with a liberal arts background and hold a master's degree or equivalent from a program that combines academic and professional preparation in library and information science, education, management, media, communications theory, and technology. The academic program of study includes some directed field experience in a library media program, coordinated by a faculty member in cooperation with an experienced library media specialist. Library media specialists meet state certification requirements for both the library media specialist and professional educator classifications. While there may be many practicing library media specialists who have only an undergraduate degree and whose job performance is outstanding, the master's degree is considered the entry-level degree for the profession.

The graduate degree is earned at colleges and universities whose programs are accredited by appropriate bodies such as the American Library Association (ALA), the National Council for the Accreditation of Teacher Education (NCATE), or state education agencies.

This appendix is reprinted from the American Association of School Librarians Electronic Library published in Chicago in 1995 by the American Library Association.

Appendix F

AASL Position Statement on Resource-Based Instruction: Role of the School Library Media Specialist in the Whole Language Approach

The whole language program is a process for developing literacy by integrating oral and written language experiences into the literature and content areas. Spoken language, reading, and writing are learned simultaneously. Through this holistic approach, with students reading "real books" and writing for the purpose of communicating, learning becomes relevant, interesting, and motivational and prepares students for life-long learning. Acquisition, organization, and dissemination of resources to support the whole language program through the library media center is cost-effective for the entire school district.

The following elements are integral to an effective whole language program:

- The library media center is flexibly scheduled so that students and teachers have unlimited physical and intellectual access to a wide range of materials. Students are not limited to using only commercially prescribed or teacher-selected materials.

This appendix is reprinted from the American Association of School Librarians Electronic Library published in Chicago in 1995 by the American Library Association.

- Students choose from a varied, non-graded collection of materials which reflect their personal interests.
- Students learn to identify, analyze, and synthesize information by using a variety of materials in a variety of formats.
- Multidisciplinary approaches to teaching and learning are encouraged.
- Teachers and library media specialists cooperatively select materials and collaboratively plan activities that offer students an integrated approach to learning.
- Teachers and library media specialists share responsibility for reading and information skill instruction. They plan and teach cooperatively based on the needs of the student.
- Continual staff development is critical to whole language instruction.

The responsibility for successful implementation of whole language is shared by the entire school community; teachers, library media specialists, and administrators working together.

Appendix G

AASL Position Statement on the Role of the Library Media Specialist in Outcomes-Based Education

The library media specialist has an essential role in curriculum development. Outcomes-based education is a curriculum practice which establishes clearly defined learner outcomes based on the premise that all students can be successful learners. High expectation outcomes, which are essential for success after graduation, require carefully aligned curriculum, instructional strategies, and performance-based assessment. In their unique roles as information specialist, teacher, and instructional consultant, library media specialists actively participate in both the planning and implementation of outcomes-based education.

As information specialist, the library media specialist working collaboratively with teachers, administrators, and parents:

- provides knowledge of availability and suitability of information resources to support curriculum initiatives;
- engages in the developmental process with the planning team, using knowledge of school curriculum and professional resources;
- facilitates the use of presentation tools in print, technology, and media for dissemination efforts;

This appendix is reprinted from the American Association of School Librarians Electronic Library published in Chicago in 1995 by the American Library Association.

- serves as an expert in organizing, synthesizing, and communicating information.

As Teacher:

- determines learning outcomes, including those in information literacy, for all students in the school and/or system;
- plans, implements, and evaluates resource-based learning;
- integrates information literacy into all curriculum outcomes;
- develops on-going performanced-based assessments for determining the achievement of outcomes.

As Instructional Consultant:

- facilitates development of teachers' understanding and implementation of outcomes-based education;
- plans for learning environments supportive of curriculum integration;
- previews and selects resources and technology to accommodate the learning styles and multiple intelligences of students;
- designs and implements a variety of instructional strategies and experiences that engage each student in successful learning.

Information Power: Guidelines for School Library Media Programs

[This document] states that "the mission of the library media program is to ensure that students and staff are effective users of ideas and information." The school library media specialist is a powerful partner in providing an integrative curriculum that prepares students for success in the twenty-first century.

Scenarios of the Library Media Specialist in Outcomes-Based Education

Library media specialists actively participate in the planning and implementation of outcomes-based education as information specialists, teachers, and instructional consultants. In the following scenarios, library media specialists demonstrate these essential roles.

The Library Media Specialist as Information Specialist

Scenario #1—A library media specialist, recently appointed to the school district's new Outcomes-Based Education Committee, returning to the library media center goes "on-line" to locate information sources on this new curriculum initiative. After assessing the suitability of accumulated resources, the library media specialist selects three full-text articles to copy for the committee members and prepares an annotated bibliography of additional resources.

Scenario #2—A library media specialist, and two other members of the Outcomes-Based Education Committee, are working together to prepare a presentation for a public hearing on the outcomes proposed by the committee. After some discussion, the group decides to use a variety of media to communicate their outcomes proposal. The library media specialist has assembled a number of resources, which can be used for the presentation. Working together, the three teachers select appropriate text, audio, and visuals for their multimedia presentation.

The Library Media Specialist as Teacher

Scenario #1—A library media specialist, as a member of the K–8 science curriculum writing team, is meeting with the group to identify the information literacy outcomes that will become part of the science curriculum. After reviewing the learning outcomes of the library media department, the team decides to integrate information literacy skills into the study of an estuary. The team asks the library media specialist to work with other team members to prepare suitable examples to be incorporated into the curriculum document.

Scenario #2—A library media specialist and an English teacher are meeting with a class of high school students to evaluate video projects recently completed by the class under the guidance of the library media specialist. The videos are being used as a part of the assessment of an extensive research project on contemporary American authors. Later, the two teachers will meet to discuss and evaluate the process the students used to complete their projects.

The Library Media Specialist as Instructional Consultant

Scenario #1—A library media specialist is meeting with the middle school social studies department to determine the resources needed for their recently developed "outcomes" curriculum. Suggestions are given for the use of primary sources in several units, and a variety of multimedia programs which "fit" and demonstrate the desired outcomes. Annotated bibliographies of other available resources and examples of assessment products are provided.

Scenario #2—A library media specialist, after reviewing the new curriculum documents and soliciting input from the faculty, meets with the school administrator to discuss the need to provide a wider variety of learning environments within the library media center. A tentative long-range plan has been prepared which would add additional resources, in a wide variety of formats, to the library media collection. In addition, a floor-plan providing more space for production of materials needed for assessment is presented. The administrator, while agreeing in principle with the plan, expresses concern about fiscal constraints; both agree to investigate grant possibilities.

Appendix H
AASL Position Statement on the Role of the School Library Media Program

School library media specialists have a broad undergraduate education with a liberal arts background and hold a master's degree or equivalent from a program that combines academic and professional preparation in library and information science, education, management, media, communications theory, and technology. The academic program of study includes some directed field experience in a library media program, coordinated by a faculty member in cooperation with an experienced library media specialist. Library media specialists meet state certification requirements for both the library media specialist and professional educator classifications. While there may be many practicing library media specialists who have only an undergraduate degree and whose job performance is outstanding, the master's degree is considered the entry-level degree for the profession.

The graduate degree is earned at colleges and universities whose programs are accredited by appropriate bodies such as the American Library Association (ALA), the National Council for the Accreditation of Teacher Education (NCATE), or state education agencies.

This appendix is reprinted from the American Association of School Librarians Electronic Library published in Chicago in 1995 by the American Library Association.

Appendix I

AASL Position Statement on the Value of Library Media Programs in Education

School library media specialists are an integral part of the total educational team which prepares students to become responsible citizens in a changing global society. In today's information age, an individual's success, even existence, depends largely on the ability to access, evaluate, and utilize information. Library media specialists are leaders in carrying out the school's instructional program through their separate but overlapping roles of information specialist, teacher, and instructional consultant.

The GOALS 2000 challenge our nation to make education a top priority in preparing students to compete in the worldwide marketplace and make informed decisions about problems facing society. To guarantee every young person an equal and effective educational opportunity, officials must provide each school with library media facilities and resources to meet curriculum needs. Officials must also ensure that each school's staff includes library media professionals and support personnel to carry out the mission of the instructional program.

The American Association of School Librarians is committed to the development and improvement of strong library media programs in all schools. The ability to locate and use information in solving problems,

This appendix is reprinted from the American Association of School Librarians Electronic Library published in Chicago in 1995 by the American Library Association.

expanding ideas, and becoming informed citizens depends on access to adequate library media facilities, appropriate resources, and qualified personnel. Recent studies, such as the *Impact of School Library Media Centers on Academic Achievement,* show a strong positive correlation between library media programs and student achievement.

The American Association of School Librarians urges all administrators, teachers, school board members, parents, and community members to recognize the power of information and the critical need for strong professionally staffed library media programs so all students become effective users of information.

Appendix J
Sample Library Media Selection Policy

The selection philosophy of the Princely Public Schools' Library Media Centers is to provide a wide range of learning resources at varying levels of difficulty with diversity of appeal and presentation of different points of view to meet the needs of our community of learners. The library media specialist is charged with providing leadership and expertise—both necessary to assure that the school's library media program is an integral part of the school's instruction program.

It is the belief of Princely Public Schools that no document is final but rather evolutionary. As such, the selection policy that follows will be reviewed and revised periodically.

Introduction

The selection policy that follows reflects and supports the principles of Intellectual Freedom described in the Library Bill of Rights (ALA), Freedom to Read (ALA and AAP), Access to Resources and Services in the School Library Media Program: An Interpretation of the Library Bill of Rights (AASL), and the Statement on Intellectual Freedom (AECT). Copies of these documents may be found at each of the school library media centers in Princely and also in the offices of the district library media supervisor.

This appendix is reprinted from the American Association of School Librarians Electronic Library published in Chicago in 1995 by the American Library Association.

Objectives of Selection

1. Each individual school holds the responsibility for building its collection to meet the needs and interests of its community of learners, including students, faculty, families, and staff.
2. In selecting information resources the library media specialist and the community of learners must consider both the internal holdings and those newly available information services. This is to guarantee that newer forms of technology and information sources be incorporated at the appropriate time and in accordance with curricular needs.
3. Each school is responsible for the selection of materials for the library media collection, by purchase, gift, or local production. The selection of materials follows established Princely Public School Department budget and ordering procedures as well as state and national guidelines.
4. The library media specialist must systematically conduct a needs assessment and evaluate the collection through such means as collection mapping, to assure that resources are selected and removed according to the principles of intellectual freedom. Care must be taken to provide students with access to information that represents diverse points of view in a pluralistic society.

Responsibility for Selection of Learning Resources

The Princely Public School Board delegates the responsibility for the selection of learning resources to the professional staff employed by the school system. The district library media supervisor sets acquisition processes including ordering procedures and processing of all materials. Collection development planning occurs at the school level.

While selection of learning resources involves many people (library media specialists, teachers, administrators, students, family members, and community persons), the responsibility for coordinating the selection of materials and making the recommendations for purchase rests with the library media specialist and the professional personnel at the building and district levels.

Criteria for Selection

1. Resources shall support and be consistent with the mission and goals of the Princely Public School Department and the aims and objectives of individual schools and specific curricula.
2. Learning resources shall meet high standards of quality in content and presentation.
3. Learning resources shall be appropriate for the subject area and for the age and developmental levels of the intended audience.
4. Learning resources shall have aesthetic, literary, and/or social values.
5. Physical format and appearance of learning resources shall be suitable for their intended use.
6. Learning resources shall be designed to help the community of learners gain an awareness, appreciation, and knowledge of our diverse society.
7. Learning resources shall be designed to motivate students and staff to examine their own attitudes and behaviors so they may comprehend their own duties, responsibilities, rights, and privileges in relationship to the world around them.
8. Learning resources shall be selected for their strengths rather than rejected for their weaknesses.
9. Learning resources shall be selected to promote a balanced collection that should include opposing viewpoints on various issues, beliefs, and practices.

Questions

1. Does this document provide general guidelines for the selection of all materials or just for library materials?
2. Can it be used for both? Why or why not?
3. Are the objectives for the selection of materials clearly stated? How can they be improved?
4. Are the lines of authority and responsibility clearly defined?
5. Do you agree that each school should select/build for their school? If Princely is an urban area is this cost effective? Should this section speak to cooperative collection development?

6. Although the policy refers to materials in various formats, should there be something specific for online products and searches that are printed out for student use?
7. Are the guidelines for selection and reevaluation of titles in the existing collection clear? Should they be more specific? Should they be modified? How so?

Appendix K
Sample Library Media Policy for Reevaluation of Selected Materials

From time to time, the suitability of particular print and nonprint materials may be questioned. The principles of freedom and professional selection must be adhered to, and the school will have no obligation to remove questioned material from use before or during a review process. If materials are questioned, the following procedure, based upon the American Library Association's national accepted policies, will be followed.

1. The requestor will submit his or her concerns in writing using the attached form called *Request for Reconsideration of Library/Media Center Materials*. This form will be available in any of the following locations: the school principal's office, the office of the school library media specialist, the office of the district library media supervisor. Upon receipt of the completed form the building principal will notify the district library media supervisor as well as either the assistant superintendent for Elementary Schools or the assistant superintendent for Secondary Schools (whichever is most appropriate) of the challenge.
2. The questioned material will then be reviewed by a committee of five members appointed by the building principal and his or her designee. This committee will be known as the review committee and be composed of the following building personnel:

This appendix is reprinted from the American Association of School Librarians Electronic Library published in Chicago in 1995 by the American Library Association.

- The library media specialist
- Not more than two teachers
- The principal
- Not more than two parents from the building involved

3. The Review Committee will

    - Examine the material in its entirety.
    - Read reviews of the challenged material and investigate the acceptance of this material by other professional educators.
    - Judge the material for its strength and value as a whole and not in part—the impact of the entire work often being more important than isolated words, phrases, or incidents.
    - Submit a written report of their recommendations to the building principal with copies to the district library media supervisor and the appropriate assistant superintendent.

4. The principal will notify the requester of the decision of the review committee. This will be done in writing within 30 days of receipt of the complaint.
5. If the requester is not satisfied with the review committee's decision, he or she may file a written appeal to the School Board. The School Board will consider the recommendations of the review committee and in consultation with the school board attorney, render a decision. This decision as to the suitability of the questioned material(s) will be made within 45 days of receiving the request for appeal. The School Board's decision will be the final decision within the Princely Public Schools.

Request for Reconsideration of Library Media Materials
Princely Public School Department

SCHOOL ______________________________

REQUEST MADE BY ______________________

STREET ADDRESS _______________________

CITY/STATE ______________________ ZIP ____________

TELEPHONE ____

REPRESENTING ____________________________________

PLEASE CHECK TYPE OF MATERIAL

___BOOK ____ PERIODICAL ___KIT

____AUDIO CASSETTE ____RECORD ___FILM

____ VIDEO CASSETTE ___ FILMSTRIP ___ PAMPHLET

____OTHER (BE SPECIFIC) _________________________

____

TITLE: ____

AUTHOR: ______________________________________

PUBLISHER ____________________________________

OTHER INFORMATION FROM THE ITEM ____________

The following questions are to be answered by the Requester. If sufficient space is not provided, attached additional sheets. Please sign your name and date each of the attachments you supply.

1. DID YOU READ, LISTEN TO, OR VIEW THE ENTIRE WORK?

   ___ YES ___NO ___ IF NO, WHICH SECTIONS?

2. TO WHAT IN THE MATERIAL DO YOU OBJECT? BE SPECIFIC, CITING PAGES, FRAMES IN A FILMSTRIP, FILM SEQUENCES AND SO ON.

____

3. WHAT DO YOU BELIEVE IS THE THEME OR PURPOSE OF THIS MATERIAL?

____

4. DO YOU FEEL THERE IS ANYTHING OF VALUE IN THIS MATERIAL?

____

____

5. WHAT DO YOU FEEL MIGHT BE THE RESULT OF A STUDENT USING THIS MATERIAL?

____

6. FOR WHAT AGE GROUP WOULD YOU RECOMMEND USING THIS MATERIAL?

____

7. HAVE YOU HAD THE OPPORTUNITY TO REVIEW THE EVALUATIONS OF THIS MATERIAL BY PROFESSIONAL CRITICS? _____ NO _____ YES

____

8. IF YOU HAVE ANSWERED YES TO NUMBER 7, PLEASE LIST THE REVIEW YOU HAVE READ.

____

____

9. WHAT DO YOU WANT THE SCHOOL TO DO ABOUT THIS WORK?
   _____ DO NOT ASSIGN OR RECOMMEND IT TO MY CHILD
   _____ WITHDRAW IT FROM ALL STUDENTS
   _____ SEND IT BACK TO THE LIBRARY MEDIA SPECIALIST FOR RE-EVALUATION
   _____ OTHER (BE SPECIFIC)

____

10. WHAT WORK OF SIMILAR VALUE, CONTENT, AND FORMAT WOULD YOU SUGGEST TO REPLACE THIS MATERIAL?

____

PLEASE SIGN AND DATE THIS FORM AND RETURN IT TO THE PERSON WHO GAVE IT TO YOU.

____

YOUR NAME DATE

Questions

1. By having the requestor submit everything in writing, are they limiting complaints to the more literate members of the community?
2. Should there be a vehicle for interviewing the requestor?
3. Should the deliberations of the review committee be open?
4. Why is the school board attorney involved only at the level of the School Board? Is it necessary that this person be involved from the beginning?
5. Should this procedure and the form be available in other languages?
6. Should there be an advocate for the requestor who can provide translation service?
7. Should there be a statement made to the requestor prior to the meeting of the review committee regarding why this material was added to the collection?

Suggested Readings

American Association of School Librarians and Association for Educational Communications and Technology. *Information Power: Guidelines for School Library Media Programs*. Chicago: ALA, 1988.

Lance, Keith Curry, et al. *The Impact of School Library Media Centers on Academic Achievement.* Castle Rock, Colo.: Hi Willow Research & Publishing, 1993.

"Restructuring and School Libraries." (Special Section) *NASSP Bulletin* 75 (May 1991): 1–58. (A Special Section on the School Library for the Nineties). *Phi Delta Kappan* 73 (March 1992): 521–37.

Stripling, Barbara K. *Libraries for the National Education Goals.* Syracuse, N.Y.: ERIC Clearinghouse on Information Resources, Syracuse University, 1992.

Works Cited

1. *Encarta*. Redmond, Wash.: Microsoft, 1996.
2. *Infotrac*. Foster City, Calif.: Information Access, 1991– .

Selected Bibliography

American Association of School Librarians and Association for Educational Communications and Technology. *Information Power: Guidelines for School Library Media Programs*. Chicago: American Library Association, 1988.

Anderson, Pauline H. *Planning School Library Media Facilities*. Hamden, Conn.: Library Professional Publications, 1990.

Assessment and the School Library Media Center. Editors: Carol Collier Kuhlthau, et al. Englewood, Colo.: Libraries Unlimited, 1994.

Belcher, Jane C. and Julia M. Jacobson. *From Idea to Funded Project*. 4th ed. Phoenix, Ariz.: Oryx, 1992.

Biagini, Mary Kay. *A Model for Problem Solving and Decision Making: Managing School Library Media Programs*. Englewood, Colo.: Libraries Unlimited, 1988.

Buchanan, Jan. *Flexible Access Library Media Programs*. Englewood, Colo.: Libraries Unlimited, 1991.

Cleaver, Betty P. and William D. Taylor. *The Instructional Consultant Role of the Library Media Specialist*. Chicago: American Library Association, 1989.

Doll, Carol Ann and Pamela Barron. *Collection Analysis for the School Library Media Center: A Practical Approach*. Chicago: American Library Association, 1990.

Edsall, Marian S. *Practical PR for School Library Media Centers*. New York: Neal-Schuman, 1984.

Eisenberg, Michael B. *Curriculum Initiative: An Agenda and Strategy for Library Media Programs*. Norwood, N.J.: Ablex, 1988.

Haycock, Ken. *The School Library Program in the Curriculum*. Englewood, Colo.: Libraries Unlimited, 1990.

Instructional Technology: Past, Present, and Future. 2nd edition. Editor: Gary Anglin. Englewood, Colo.: Libraries Unlimited, 1994.

Lance, Kevin Curry, et al. *Impact of School Library Media Centers on Academic Achievement*. Castle Rock, Colo.: Hi Willow Research, 1993.

Loertscher, David V. *Taxonomies of the School Library Media Program*. Englewood, Colo.: Libraries Unlimited, 1988.

Morris, Betty J., John T. Gillespie, and Diana L. Spirt. *Administering the School Library Media Center*. New York: Bowker, 1992.

O'Neil, Rosanna M. *Total Quality Management in Libraries: A Sourcebook*. Englewood, Colo.: Libraries Unlimited, 1994.

Prostano, Ernest T. and J. S. Prostano. *The School Library Media Center*. Englewood, Colo.: Libraries Unlimited, 1987.

Renewal at the Schoolhouse: Management Ideas for Library Media Specialists and Administrators. Edited by Ben B. Caron and Jane Bandy Smith. Englewood, Colo.: Libraries Unlimited, 1993.

Salmon, Sheila, et al. *Power Up Your Library: Creating the New Elementary School Library Program*. Englewood, Colo.: Libraries Unlimited, 1996.

School Library Management Notebook. Worthington, Ohio: Linworth, 1994.

School Library Media Annual, 1995. Volume 13: The Future of School Libraries. Editor: Betty J. Morris et al. Englewood, Colo.: Libraries Unlimited, 1995.

Sherman, Steve. *ABC's of Library Promotion*. 3rd ed. Metuchen, N.J.: Scarecrow, 1992.

Stein, Barbara L. and Risa W. Brown. *Running a School Library Media Center*. New York: Neal-Schuman, 1992.

Stueart, Robert D. and John Taylor Eastlick. *Library Management*. 4th ed. Englewood, Colo.: Libraries Unlimited, 1993.

Sutton, Dave. *So You're Going to Run a Library: A Library Management Primer*. Englewood, Colo.: Libraries Unlimited, 1995.

Vleck, Charles. W. and Raymond V. Wiman. *Managing Media Services: Theory and Practice*. Englewood, Colo.: Libraries Unlimited, 1989.

Walster, Dian. *Managing Time: A How-to-Do-It Manual for School and Public Libraries*. New York: Neal-Schuman, 1993.

Woolls, Blanche. *Grant Proposal Writing: A Handbook for School Library Media Specialists*. New York: Greenwood Press, 1986.

Woolls, Blanche. *Managing School Library Media Programs*. Englewood, Colo.: Libraries Unlimited, 1988.

Woolls, Blanche. *The School Library Media Manager*. Englewood, Colo.: Libraries Unlimited, 1994.

Woolls, Blanche. *Supervision of District Level Library Media Programs*. Englewood, Colo.: Libraries Unlimited, 1990.

Index

Numbers refer to the first page of the case study or appendix.

About the Authors

AMY G. JOB (M.L.S., Rutgers University; M.Ed., Montclair University; Ed.D., Seton Hall University) is a librarian and an instructor and coordinator of the program for educational media specialists at William Paterson University, Wayne, New Jersey. She has received the Distinguished Service Award of the College and University/ACRL New Jersey Section and has published several articles in professional journals and recently authored the New Jersey section of *Exploring the Northeast States Through Literature* (Oryx Press, 1994). She is coauthor of *Reference Work in School Library Media Centers: A Book of Case Studies* (Scarecrow, 1996).

MARYKAY W. SCHNARE (M.B.A., University of Connecticut; M.L.S., the University of Pittsburgh) is the library media specialist for Nathan Bishop Middle School in Providence, Rhode Island. She was 1996 Rhode Island Teacher of the Year and is president-elect of the Rhode Island Educational Media Association. She was named the 1997/98 Milken Family Foundation National Educator. She is coauthor of *Reference Work in School Library Media Centers: A Book of Case Studies* (Scarecrow, 1996).